BreatheYourOMBalance
Yoga and Our Relationships

Volume Three

Introduced by
Sarah Michelle

Series Editors
Kitty Madden and Shana Thornton

Volume Three Editor
Beverly Fisher

Thorncraft Publishing
Clarksville, Tennessee

ISBN-13: 978-0-9979687-6-7
ISBN-10: 0-9979687-6-1

Cover Design by etcetera...
Cover photo by Amanda Blount Photography
Cover models, Sarah Michelle, Ryan Kelly, and Hailey Kelly

Library of Congress Control Number: 2021930401

Thorncraft Publishing
Clarksville, TN
http://www.thorncraftpublishing.com
thorncraftpublishing@gmail.com

10 9 8 7 6 5 4 3 2 1

CONTENTS

FOREWORD
By Shana Thornton

Before 2020 was a reality, back in late 2018, I sent out a call asking for writings about our relationships and how a yoga practice might have altered yours.

During the time that I was compiling this book, I was working with a local high school media arts program to design a brochure that highlights African American culture and leadership within the town where I live and work, in Clarksville, Tennessee, where I publish all of Thorncraft's books. While I publish work from authors who live all over the world, I also want to give back to my community by creating works with my publishing company's talents and skills.

In 2016, I also started teaching a seasonal yoga session at Dunbar Cave State Park. Most of the classes are scheduled at sunset, surrounded by candlelight, and take place at the mouth of the cave. I talk about the indigenous artwork and history of the cave, linking the natural forms of asana, physical yoga postures, to the forms of nature. One of the images in the cave is described as a "warrior lying down" by some of the tour guides. I connect those images in the cave, including the warrior lying down, to the warriors (*virabhadrasana*) within yoga, as well as *savasana*, final relaxation. These connections lead to a practice honoring *pranayama* (breath work) and meditation at this local sacred site. I donate the proceeds from the yoga sessions to the state park.

When the pandemic arrived, we decided to put the yoga classes on pause. This book was in a holding place as well. I stopped to consider the relationships within my life that connected to my community—books and yoga, the written work and the sacred movement of body, the concentration and mindfulness required in all of these expressions.

The #BlackLivesMatter Movement called everyone to action, acknowledging the literal and symbolic need to breathe collectively, to acknowledge that Black Lives were being robbed of breath and, thus, life, and that the Black community deserved positive change so that we might all be deserving of change.

I received a few messages from contributors during this time, asking if they could write more, considering what we have been through in 2020. With a theme of Yoga and Relationships, I knew that the book needed to include writings that were representations of what we recently experienced, while retaining the writings prior to 2020.

Collectively, these expressions of yoga and relationships reveal the sacred connection we have to one another now, across time and space. We often reach back through the mists of time in our practices to connect with ancestors, to acknowledge the hard work in creating community that was put in before us, to learn about people whose lives were different than our own, and we often glimpse into the future toward a hope of connection in honoring our varied experiences and backgrounds. This book provides a reach back to our past selves with writings from before the pandemic and the book shows a glimpse into that hope as well, toward people who believe in the power of connection and community to heal and transform our world.

BreatheYourOMBalance

Yoga and Our Relationships
Volume Three

INTRODUCTION
By Sarah Michelle

Sometimes we don't understand how different our perception is until we have seen things from another perspective. Like many others, I grew up in a traumatic environment, I operated in survival mode and it clouded my point of view in ways that I didn't realize until I began to look back. When I came to my first yoga class I was wearing my grief, unprocessed emotions and automatic responses like armor. I did not realize I was using my past perceptions to keep everyone at arm's length, recreating the emotional climate of my past. I opened a door with yoga, one that I had long forgotten even existed. When the skeletons came tumbling out in cascades of memories, unconscious behaviors, and self destructive choices, it was that perspective that fueled my community growth.

I began to cultivate relationships with others that were healing from similar traumas, bonding over our similarities, and sometimes burning bridges because of our differences. Some friends were rapid lessons in growth, illuminating the things I needed to change in order to move forward; and others have integrated into my life becoming family to me. It was these interconnected spaces that allowed me to see beyond the veil of illusion feeding my anxiety.

The *BreatheYourOMBalance* series is a collection of stories similar to mine, of the traumas and the healing, the bumps and bruises, the smiles and tears along the way. The third edition illuminates yoga's impact on these relationships and how community can be cultivated through the simplicity of breath, movement, sound, and stillness.

The magic of how these communities grow, the synchronicities between us, and the depth of the bonds formed is still mystifying to me. In my practice, I feel the significance of relationship is honored through the phrase "Namaste." It's a depth of understanding that the light of life is within us all. No matter our outward or inward appearances, we can view each relationship, each interaction, as an extension of ourselves.

This is not to excuse abuses, or promote hanging on to relationships that are hurting us, but to understand that each individual is shaped by their own closet of circumstances and may very well be wearing a piece of armor that once adorned your fragile spirit. Likely, they too are holding onto pain that causes them to react, but by being honest and authentic with each other, we can begin to reflect light after we've acknowledged our shadows in the stillness and silence of meditation. Initially, we may do this solely for our own peace, but as a collective, we begin to find freedom from the weight of emotional repression.

When I say "namaste," I am acknowledging the pure humanity that exists within all of us, before the closet doors were even built, before any circumstance clouded our perception, the place of being. I am affirming that I can empathize with you without saying a single word simply because we share the common human thread. It is through the connection of our experiences along our journey we begin to gain wisdom and consciously evolve. It's honestly acknowledging our personal thoughts, feelings and emotions, taking accountability, and holding the awareness that every single human being has the potential to experience the same. This is my secret to cultivating compassion for others and it is my prayer that others may find the healing that this state of being offers. It is the truth of unconditional love, and I learned it through the relationships knitted and weaved together over the course of my journey.

I experience it in the genuine warmth of my children's embrace, the unified sound of a group breathing as one, the tears of understanding reflected in the eyes of a friend, the heart-wrenching moment when you understand that someone else has also felt sharp edges of grief. There is a weighted significance to yoga on the mat, but it's the way we move in this world that truly matters.

Yoga offers us a guidebook toward separating the self from experiences and unifying the self with the Divine self that we all share. I have come to understand that yoga isn't simply movement, but "a movement." A movement of self-realization sparked within a collective of souls. If you want to grow anything, you must start with the earth, the soil with which your seed will grow. Here is to cultivating healthy, fertile soil for our humanness to grow compassionately and unapologetically, allowing our roots to form a network of understanding.

As you read through these pages, I invite you to explore the feelings inspired within you honestly and openly, and allow yourself to feel the thread of relationship with someone who in reality is a stranger, but feels like an old friend. If an excerpt inspires an emotional reaction, consider pausing to reflect on your connection with the soul who so graciously invited you into a piece of their life.

The words in this book are patient enough to wait, and I invite you to take your time with yourself to realize how intertwined we all truly are. My sincerest hope is that these words of connection, hope and the will to carry on will help readers find faith in their own ability to just BE. As human Beings, I believe this is our Divine right. Namaste, sweet soul. I am grateful to have community with you.

Thorncraft

BreatheYourOMBalance
Yoga and Our Relationships

The Beginning
Poetry by Yvette Huber

Seize strategic floor space in the back.
Press the mat down to define territorial borders.
But an inconsistent practice is exposed
When the rubber frontline rolls back in retreat.

Command the body to stay still during vigil.
Watch and wait, but boredom creeps in.
Lower the gaze to feign a meditative expression,
Yet remain wary of all who enter the room.

An invading mat snaps open with the flick of a wrist,
Stirring the dust of discomfort as it lands nearby.
Trespassing toes advance in the periphery.
These moments before class are interminable.

So how did it start? Don't remember. Does it matter?
The smile, the whisper, the giggle,
The unexpected escalation of connection,
The tickle of friendship across the heart.

An admonishing "Shh!" ceases the exchange,
But only temporarily.
A wall of isolation is crumbling
As the yoga is finally starting.

Rise tall in Mountain Pose.
And from this vantage point, in awe.
For even in a darkened room,
Light reaches around shadows to touch everyone.

On Memory
Poetry by Jesse Curran

This morning as we closed our eyes
resting on the beach at the end of our practice
my hand found yours as it has these past years.
And though it was the time for no thinking
I thought of Japan and Hayama and that promontory
projecting into the Pacific, its soft sandy grasses
and that welcome relief, the feeling
of fleeing Tokyo in August
to salute the sun
in the land where it rises.
It was the tender time of early love
of cocktails, jellyfish stings
and the self's steady unraveling
into the idea of the other.
But that week in Hayama
was mainly those mornings
the shoulder strengthening
and the back bend finally found.
And though I had already left
and was home by then, drifting
through jet lag, laundry, loneliness
there was this sense
that you had changed me
and would continue to
for many years to come.
Key West, New York, Hayama:
in the time for no thinking
I keep thinking
how this ocean is that one
how its extent binds our distance
how this practice connects us
how this need not be my memory
to be ours

Forget-me-nots
Father on the River
For K
Poetry by Mitzi Cross

Her father summoned
me in my dream. His voice
pulling me like a kite
as I sailed
into her driveway
that morning.

When I walked up
I could see that the woman
had slipped away and there
she was, a young girl
I'd never met.

"I don't know what is going on with me," she said.

Her posture was deflated
as we started in mountain
and moved slowly through
sun salutation to warm
our bodies. With the last exhale
she climbed onto the healing table.

We set our intention
as my hands moved like a divining-
rod searching for her water. I closed
my eyes to see inside, and there it was,
a fissure, a tiny purple knot tied
to each side of her heart, pulled
taut to close the wound. I pulled at the
the thread until I felt it loosen.

"Deep breath. Inhale...
one, two, three. Now exhale."

Her tummy trembled
beneath my warm palms
as I spiraled counterclockwise
to open, to unwind.

We breathed together
until we found union and
a quiet whimper escaped
her lips then I heard
a loud pop, then another and another,
like a band of belts bursting open
across her chest.

Her breath stuttered in her throat
caught like a trapped hummingbird
fluttering to escape.

 "Now push it out as you exhale."

In all the years I'd never seen her cry,
but an ancient pain tidaled
through her body.

A presence cut through
my antenna, like a radio trying to tune
into a station. I held my hand
against her occipital lobe;
the mouth of God
and I stood on one foot
meditating between two channels.
It was her father, riding down
a swift river, trying hard to make
contact. My teeth chattered with the taste
of aluminum. My skin was sticky
and cold and his words poured
from my mouth as he sailed past us.

"You couldn't have saved me
even with all your training," he said.

His words rippled over the rocky

wake of the river gathering current
right before entering her body,
sending her cries echoing across the sky.
A lifetime of guilt poured
out of her as she forced her breath
through her tears. I kissed her forehead.

"Breathe with me," I said
as a light mist cleansed
the air and I watched
her return with eyes as
clear as rain water and
soft as forget-me-nots.

Downward, Old Dog
Nonfiction by Barry Kitterman

I was a few months shy of my sixtieth birthday when I discovered yoga.

That isn't exactly right. I've known about yoga for a long time. My wife, Jill, has been doing yoga for _____ years. Her middle name is Kundalini. She knew Iyengar personally. He used to drive an ice cream truck through her neighborhood—Miller, Indiana—when she was a little girl. In the summer time. Something like that.

I only started *practicing* yoga a few years ago. My new friend David Jones (no, not that Davey Jones, not the other one either) was teaching a restorative class, and I was ready for restoration. Maybe I was sixty, but one of my knees was going on seventy-five. My hamstrings had once been compared, uncharitably, to rebar. And I was on the verge of a 2/3 life crisis. Responsibilities falling down like rain. Aging parents. Children fleeing the nest. My dog bit my best friend's wife. Good lord. I was ready for yoga.

I remember my first day of class. I couldn't touch my toes, and I felt lost without my glasses. My T-shirt wouldn't stay tucked in. My arms were heavy. I was really thirsty. All of that before I came out of the dressing room.

Once in the actual studio, my relationship with yoga was different from what I'd thought it would be. (This is how I was encouraged to think: I had a relationship with yoga, like yoga was an old squeeze from my bohemian days.) For one thing, I'd had an unreasonable fear if I lay down on a yoga mat, I would need help from the others to get back up. I put that fear to rest. Oh, those others. I was told not to pay attention to anyone else in the room, not to compare myself to the rest. But I couldn't help it. I was older than most of them, lots older than some. I was less symmetrical, more hard-of-hearing, and the sweat poured off me like I was the *before* guy in a deodorant commercial. My new friends, by comparison, looked comfortable. In a yoga class, women don't sweat much, not really. Everyone else in that assembly of yogis knew all the poses. They knew the lingo. Many of them had been speaking Sanskrit from a tender age.

I tried my best to keep up, and I was grateful, as I have always been grateful, for my wife's loving encouragement. I was also grateful that Jill had not placed her mat next to mine at the beginning of class. ("Are you ok?" I could imagine her saying. "That's a funny color you're turning. Don't worry about all the sweat. I'm sure this place has a shop-vac ....")

In that first session, a lesser man would have abandoned his post, but I stayed in the room. I did most of the poses, the *asanas*. I did several asanas nobody had ever done before. I mopped my brow with my towel and I drank all my water, and then I kind of wished I hadn't drunk all that water. I had cleverly left my wristwatch in the dressing room, and I did not try to check the time, not even once.

At the end of the hour, I discovered there is a payoff to every yoga class worth its salt, a finale, a *coup de grace*: the aptly-named corpse pose. Wherein an old guy finally stops trying to look lively and lets himself collapse in a giant heap of release. To my dismay, I also discovered I couldn't lie on my back for more than a couple of minutes—even in a padded room with soft lights and a recorded choir of *om mani padme oms*—without feeling the pain well up through the floor from a lifetime of bicycle accidents and falling out of trees and racquetball games, and that one winter in Missoula ....

There are very few things in my life that I have tried to do only one time and then given up on. (Standing on the seat of my bicycle comes to mind. Certain automotive repairs.) So I waited a few days, and with the determination of one of those League of Justice guys, I went back for more yoga. David was a wonderful teacher, a gentle man, though he did have a weakness for putting his own foot behind his ear. I took out a membership at a studio, NBalance, and I learned that *balance* was another thing I needed to work on. My daughter bought me some nifty shorts. Jill bought me a mat of my own.

Although David will always have a special place in my yoga heart, I gave other teachers a try. In the yoga world, there are many teachers named Sarah, and many named Jane. And at least one teacher named Sarah Jane. And a Julie and a Beth and a Shana. I made friends with them all. One time, on a trip to California, I did a brave thing: I went to a yoga class *in another town!*

But when I think of my yoga journey, it comes back to where it started, back to my safe place, back home. In Jill, I have the best yoga partner in the world, and each year of practice makes me see that more clearly. She recently got certified to teach, and now she lets me come to her classes where she watches out for me, though she thinks I don't know she is watching out for me. She agrees to get to the studio a few minutes early every afternoon so I can transition from creaky-old-guy to creaky-old-guy-on-his-mat. She has been known to let me use her water bottle when I forget my own. The yoga gods knew I needed such a partner, a helpmeet.

And maybe I haven't gotten a whole lot better at it but I have grown. I have been practicing regularly now for six years, and I can honestly say I have not seen anyone die in class. I have learned new ways to breathe and new ways to bend. I have nursed myself back from several non-yoga injuries. Yoga didn't cure everything. My right knee recently celebrated its eighty-sixth birthday. But yoga and swimming and acupuncture and massage and naproxen and sleeping on a wedge pillow, and staying off the roof as much as possible…it's working for me.

There are things I still long for from my yoga practice. I wish the mirrors in the studio made me look slimmer. I wish it didn't take me twice as long to get dressed after class as it takes everyone else. I wish I'd learned to play the piano.

But I love my relationship with yoga, and I can honestly say I'm okay with being the old guy in the room. If it bothers the young people, if they can't handle it, if they can't keep up, well it's just too bad for them. I'm here and I'm coming back tomorrow.

Namaste to you, too.

Mini
Poetry by Ariel Bowlin

You showed me how to tie my shoes, write my name in cursive and that
black licorice was the best.
You taught me words in Spanish and introduced me to foreign films
and Edith Piaf.
You tried to teach me to drive a car.

You took me to my first Yoga class.
It didn't really stick for either of us right then.
Years later I really fell in love with Yoga.
I don't think you ever did.

I grew up, moved away and we grew apart.
Yoga became a huge part of my life.
It is my passion and my therapy.

I encouraged you to stretch, to try a class or video.
I wanted you to take better care of yourself.
You can't really tell your parents anything though.
It doesn't work that way.

The last bond we shared was cancer.
You were diagnosed first and I wasn't far behind.
I knew I would get a flower and certificate when I finished radiation
because you had.

I was grateful for the healing yoga brought to me during that time,
And I wished that you could find that too.

Still, you had one more lesson to teach me.
You showed me the beauty of a positive attitude, optimism and hope to
the end.
It was a quiet strength.
An unspoken connection.
Like the many times we caught each other's eye to joke privately at
someone else's expense.

When you passed from this life you embedded so much of yourself in
me.
It was the final step to truly become your mini me.

I can do arm balances now.
I have beautiful leggings and a sticky mat.

The roots of my practice though are those first few classes with you.
Before yoga was popular.
Sliding on our slippery mats in our old sweat pants at the rec center.
And sharing a laugh on the drive home.

Tree Pose
Nonfiction by Khristeena Lute

I run with my pre-teen daughter through the city park. We pass lush green gardens and perfectly manicured paths, our brown ponytails bobbing together as we chat through panting breaths about her week. She tells me about her friends and their inside jokes and even the new boy she *like* likes. The sun shines brilliantly off the pond as ducks glide gracefully across the glassy surface.

Or at least, that's how I'd envisioned our run.

Instead, my daughter sat on a park bench on a cloudy day glaring at me. Both of our faces were sweaty, and our brown hair frizzed up in the humidity.

"This sucks. I'm tired. Why did you make me do this?"

We'd barely jogged half a mile.

"I can't do this. I'm terrible at it!"

"But you can't get better if you don't try and practice. And besides, we both need more time away from screens," I answered. "Come on. Race me to the other fountain. I bet I can beat you…"

"Mom…I don't *want* to try or practice. And I'm not racing you. I'm not five, anymore. You can't trick me."

"If I win, dessert tonight is fruit. If you win, ice cream," I said, giving up and offering straight-out bribery.

She shot off the park bench and sprinted down the path. I jogged slowly behind her. Maybe a little win would help her motivation.

"Ha! I won! Ice cream!" She panted, her face red. "And you'll have to get your other darling daughter to run with you. I'm not doing this again."

I sighed. Maybe not. The dream of a mother-daughter running team disappeared faster than my dreams of ever seeing my children's bedroom floors again.

Eventually, I tried again with tae kwon do. She perked up and practiced her forms in the backyard without bribery. We spent a year attending classes two times a week. I watched from the rows of parents (most of them staring at their phones) as she learned forms, kicks, and punches. Her confidence went up. *Okay,* I thought. *This is her thing. It's not my thing, but that's okay. I'm here with her. Sharing something together.*

She progressed well, and then it hit: adolescence, with its roaring self-consciousness. She found herself in a catch-22: she needed to go to class to learn her new forms, and yet…she was terrified to go to class because she didn't know her forms. Her anxiety poured off her and nearly drowned me as I tried to encourage her. Self-doubt and anxiety were the only things she found in the dojo anymore. Where is the line, as a parent, between encouraging and forcing? At what point do we, too, give up and say, *Fine, whatever?*

We moved the expensive sparring gear to the side and tried swim class at the local YMCA. Little sister hopped right in, but my older daughter hesitated. She had whined all week about not wanting to start the swim classes.

"There won't be anyone there my age! I'll feel stupid!" she had said before we left the house.

"You'll be fine. The age range is six to thirteen. You're two years under the cutoff, so I'm sure there'll be kids there of all those ages."

My husband and I watched from the sidelines. Little sister was strapped into flotation devices and was off, half doggie paddling, half just floating, and somehow, going backwards. But she grinned and splashed and happily wore herself out.

Big sister was right. She was the only older kid who couldn't swim. She was alone. She struggled to cross the pool, all the way to the deep end, with one thin boogie board held too far out to be of much use. She kicked and struggled, but she made it. She was not enjoying herself. I'd screwed up putting her in this class. As her group began to swim back across the pool, the coach motioned for her to push off the side of the pool. Instead, she pulled herself up and out of the pool and walked to me.

"I can't do it," she said simply.

"But what did the coach say? I don't understand," I started. I looked into her deep brown eyes. They glazed over a tiny bit with unshed tears. Her lower lip wobbled. "Okay. That's okay. Let's go dry off, okay?"

My husband looked at me quizzically. "It's okay," I said softly to him. "I'll figure it out."

In the locker room, she didn't say much. She changed, toweled her hair semi-dry, and packed her things into a bag.

"Mom?" I stopped spinning her swimsuit. The locker room was blissfully empty and quiet. "I'm sorry."

I pulled her suit out of the spinner and walked back to her, sitting on the bench. "Me, too. I'm proud of you for trying, though. I love you." I hugged her and kissed the top of her head, which had become more difficult now that she was my height.

The next week, little sister happily donned her swimsuit for class.

"What am I going to do?" asked big sister.

"You and I are going to take a yoga class together while Dad takes your sister to swim class," I explained. "Wear comfy clothes."

An argument ensued. "I can't! I can't do it! I don't know how!"

Something shifted in my normally low-key, meh-style of parenting. "You're going. You'll go to at least one class. With me. I'm not abandoning you, so you won't be alone. And you need to be more active and healthy! You spend all of your time sitting at school or sitting in front of a computer!"

As she stomped up the stairs, my husband whispered, "Are you sure about this fight?"

I sighed and answered, "It's too late now. I started it. If I give in, she'll smell weakness."

The air on the car ride to the Y was heavy with adolescent pouting and repeated refrains of, "Do I have to?"

And my stern replies. "Yes." Stubborn Mom versus Stubborn Daughter.

I led her to the yoga studio, hung our coats, and placed our shoes under the bench outside the studio door. I let her follow me, in silence, as we crossed the softly lit studio to the supply closet to retrieve mats, blocks, and blankets. I handed her a mat and began arranging my own things, letting her figure it out. It felt cruel to ignore her, but if I didn't, she wouldn't figure out how to do things on her own. When I glanced back, she was watching as the other class members settled their mats and adjusted themselves into a corpse pose. She copied them.

The instructor set her phone into the speaker to play typical new-age-yoga-music, and she led the group through various asanas for the full hour. I made it a point not to look at my daughter, so she couldn't plead with me with her eyes. When I did sneak a look back, she was following right along.

"And now, let's ease into a nice squatted pose, square back," the instructor said as she squatted on her own mat. "For those who feel comfortable, feel free to rock into the start of crow pose, but remember: yoga is all about knowing your own body. Don't push to discomfort. Just do what feels comfortable for each one of you." The instructor lifted herself on her hands with her knees tucked up on her elbows. Around the room, each person did some variation. Some people, like me, kept the tiniest bit of toe on the ground as we wavered back and forth. A few were able to go fully into crow, while others shook their heads and laughed. Nope. Not yet.

The music suddenly bounced into a chirpy ring tone. "Oh no! I forgot to put my phone on Do Not Disturb!" The instructor laughed. Everyone in the class laughed good-naturedly, as well. She adjusted her phone, and the new-age music kicked back on. "Go with the flow, I guess! I'll have to have my kids teach me how to use my phone! And now, let's sit back into the beginning of firefly, which is safer than crow because when you fall, and we all do, you land on your butt, instead of your face." The instructor straightened her legs over her elbows while holding herself up with her arms.

"And don't worry, if you're not ready for this pose, yet, there's lots of variations that will help build the muscle to get ready for it later on." She eased us into a few other asanas, before guiding us into standing tree pose. As the group followed her example, carefully placing the foot on the inside of the thigh, I lost my balance and set my toes back to my mat. A few others did, as well.

"And remember, it's okay to wobble. We're all different, and we all have different bodies and different strengths," the instructor said.

"You got that right!" joked a middle-aged woman in the back row. She held onto the ballet barre on the wall for balance. Everyone in the room laughed with her, as tree after tree wobbled, wavered, and tipped.

I heard a little giggle behind me.

The instructor led us through a few more slow asanas and into a deep lunge. We opened our arms up wide and tilted to look up at the ceiling.

"Now, let out a nice growl. If you've had a stressful week, let out those inner demons!"

This time, I heard a little snort of laughter from behind.

Soon, the class wrapped up. "How was it?" I asked my daughter as we pulled our shoes on outside the door.

"Not terrible."

"Will you come with me again next week?"

"Sure," she shrugged, as she pulled on her shoes and jacket.

"Good enough for me," I replied. More active lifestyle achieved and reassurance that *this* might not be the thing that sends her to therapy in her thirties. Now, if I could just find a way to get her to clean her room.

Changing Seasons
Poetry by Jessica R. Gibbs

I say goodbye to the late evening sun,
Drying my hair as I ride my bicycle back home.
Leaves now brushed yellow
By chilly, foggy mornings.
Summer's haze is gone.
The shadows grow long,
And darkness settles like a veil,
Drifting down from the sky to the ground.
As leaves coast to their grassy landing,
I shed my past.
Walking over the crackling remnants,
The winds of the changing seasons
Lift the hair from my neck.
My face welcomes the chill,
Sharpening the edges of my cheekbones,
Turning my cheeks pink with prospect.
And my face turns toward the horizon,
Ripe with the future
But chest rising,
Feeling the sharp, crisp inhale
Of the present.

Centering Key
Nonfiction and Snow Photograph by Kitty Madden
All other photography by Beverly Fisher

For me, this Tibetan centering key represents the epitome of true power. Its graceful arc, curves, and spiral are embodied in snakes, streams, and rivers. Its shapes are revered in myths like the African "Rainbow Serpent" and sacred symbols in the ancient practice of Reiki which dates back to the Bonn civilization, approximately 2500 years ago. The creek at the base of our land revealed natural springs emerging from its three curves which mimics the centering key! We like to contemplate the cascades and waterfall toward the end of our land as being akin to the arc, curves and spiral in the centering key. The fossilized corals forming this symbol are embedded with quartz crystal from ancient oceanic formations. These lithostrotion corals are between 323 and 358 million years old according to the National Park Service and are indigenous to Middle Tennessee.

The centering key is called "nin giz zida." When pronounced phonetically, we chant: ni in gee ee ee ease zee ee da. During our years of observation, we've noticed that joy and peace are often enhanced for many souls, including cats, dogs, birds, and other animals, as well as children, friends, and neighbors while they are in or near the installation. One day a handsome young meter reader approached and asked to take pictures of our centering key. It's adjacent to our water meter and he said he'd been admiring our roadside art every month and looked forward to seasonal and artistic changes. He said his other job is landscape architecture, but that no commission he was ever assigned to create was anything like our land.

We allow our intuition to guide us when people linger in a state of awe; and sometimes we offer to sing the tones accompanying the key and/or trace the symbol onto their backs or into the air.

If you'd like to try this at home, you may use your own hands on the front of your torso starting at your neck and culminating in a spiral at your root chakra. When practiced on another body, one begins drawing the arc at the base of the skull, and the hands imitate the three curves down the main energy centers of the spinal cord, ending in a spiral around the coccyx area. We usually chant the nine musical tones accompanying the centering key simultaneously; the musical notes are as follows:

D, G, D, G, B, A, G, F#, G

Northport Yoga Center
Poetry by Jesse Curran

I have been practicing hatha yoga at Northport Yoga Center since 2010; I began teaching yoga there in 2013. For many years, the studio occupied the most humble of spaces: one small, carpeted room, off of a back alley, on Main Street in Northport Village on Long Island. About two years ago, the center was in danger of losing its lease as the building recently switched hands. Serendipitously, the business owner, my beloved teacher, was able to find a new, beautiful, affordable space just down the block. While we were all very excited to move to our new home (on a second floor with big windows and wood floors!), I also felt a loss at leaving the small back-alley room that had witnessed the transformation of my being over the years. I wrote the following linked sequence of poems in order to pay homage to the space itself. It was a place that nurtured a resilient community, healthy relationships, and opened my eyes to the ways in which practices like yoga can help unsustainable places like Long Island breathe again.

A blank page
the pause at the top of the inhale
what we make between the vertebrae
what these walls create
what we hope opens
    between thoughts
what we clear
    in our schedules
what we make between our ribs as we drink
    in each breath.

this room
this place
our yoga

    space.

**

Seven years, and so
well over a thousand *savasanas*
on this faded carpet.

Just one of so many bodies
seeking surrender
down this back alleyway.

Just one lotus flower
sunk in imperfection.

This poison, this paradise
our home.

This sweet
suburban
mud.

**

In this space:
Pregnant women
Babies in bucket carseats
Young men who died too young
Wounded who healed
Many with tears
Some lovers, some husbands
Many wives, some widows
The brokenhearted and the broken boned
People just passing through
Those with no English who watched
Teenagers who came for a week
Caregivers in need of care
Teachers who are students, students
Becoming teachers
Therapists in need of silence
The stiff the stretchy
the frantic the frail
the broken the beautiful

come – this is
our studio
our *sangha,*
our center,
our home.

**

I remember the first time I met you,
though for you, I was just one of many
who walk in here searching for something.
You were already at home here, a home
you created for others. I was heartbroken,
full of fear and shame and the sadness
that strips appetite and hollows cheeks.
You helped me bring my shoulders back
and down, starting years of slow, steady work.
I didn't know then what you were doing for me.
I couldn't see then that I would learn to love
another here, that I would become tall here.
That I would train, would mourn, would risk
would teach, would breathe the best I could
into two babies here. That I would forgive
myself here, learn how to be kind
to myself here. I keep coming back to you.
Your svelte frame, your inviting eyes
Your poses far more pleasing
than those in the magazines.
A body artist at work, but
more than that,
your compassion
your kindness
this space
you create
for all of us.

**

Asana as seat,
But where does the seat sit?
The center. This center.

Our center.

**

Yes, there is a van plowing tourists
who sip sangria in Spanish cafes.

There are former bright students who studied ecology
posing as Hitler and practicing hate.

There is also a farm down the block where people just yesterday
picked eight hundred pounds of tomatoes.

There are mothers nursing their newborns
and toddlers negotiating cookies.

There is a band playing *sugar-pie honey bunch*
as people dance in the park.

The August heat breaks into thunder
and the sidewalks stream with rain.

There are strong women sinking into the earth,
in this room, surrendering
in *savasana.*

A Study of the Consequences of Heart Openers
Nonfiction by Rachael Rhee

"Always resignation and acceptance. Always prudence and honour and duty. Elinor, where is your heart?" Jane Austen, Sense and Sensibility

My father is the eldest of three sons. I am his firstborn, which makes me the matriarch of my familial generation. I sit alone in my bracket of the family tree. A tree topper, pointed, and decisive in its solitariness. The forest of our genealogy is dotted with such heads of families: my grandfather, my father, me, all bloody-minded standard bearers of emotional independence, the better to lead our families with clarity of thought and conviction. No wailing and garment rending at funerals for us. We head the procession to the grassy ancestral burial mound dry-eyed and solemn, a lone bulwark for the family's grief to break against. A consequence of birth order or being the daughter of a man who never needed an audience, I have always been good at standing in front, yet wholly apart. I have always been good at being alone.

I turn twenty-three on a cold, clear night in the Iraqi desert. We are halfway through our deployment, and the sand is wedging itself with steady persistence between our teeth and the cracks in our resolve, carefully caulked over with counting down the days and scotch-taped with gallows humor. The more isolated the outpost, the better (grimmer) the jokes. Tempers fray, because of the grittiness in our mouths, and by consequence, our words. My platoon suffers my sometimes-unpopular decisions as the January stars witness our campaign with their hard, wintry stares. I shield myself with solitude, the family tradition, to maintain perspective. I trade being one of the guys with being a strong leader. Somewhere between whispering, "happy birthday" to myself on the east watch tower that night and my friend dying wordlessly two months ago, I had become an island unto myself. I became even better at being alone.

I was blind to the depths of his despair. For all my posturing, I failed him. Or maybe I failed him because of my posturing. Who would confide in a friend that eschewed needing anything from anyone? He had left the rest of us in the desert and gone where I couldn't follow. No way to interrogate him, shield at my side for once, to ask him why.

I came home that spring and began my yogic practice to heal an overworked arm. In practice, I imagined myself as balanced as a mobile, turning so subtly to seem almost still at first, every element, every asana poised seamlessly against the next, no cracks, nowhere for sand to settle. But the practice also inspired in me a craft-like accuracy, a care for the small things of my world. The crane of a neck. The absolute stillness at the bottom of a breath. The way a heart opener creates a twisting in the chest, like grief being wrung out. The warm timbre of an instructor's voice. The problem is, sometimes things care back, like the instructor with the voice who invites you to trade ego for unconditional self-acceptance.

The invitation is a subtle, implicit byproduct of the practice. *What do you need today? How about practicing only as much as you need, for yourself only? Maybe you have everything you need, right here with you. There are no decisions to make for anyone else. Listen to your body.* Maybe, loosen your death grip on emotional discipline because your hand is starting to cramp inside the bowl of your shield. Your shield arm needs rest.

You never saw the signs because you didn't yet speak the language of loss. Maybe nothing you could have said or screamed into the sandstorm of his private anguish would have kept him alive. The winds may have stolen your words away, keeping you beyond his hearing. You'll never know, and that's okay.

You be lionheart brave, firstborn, because now, one day, you may hear your heart audibly break for the first time since last winter. Maybe, it's worth it, because joy, unalloyed, is just as profound as grief is.

Maybe, give yourself grace and mercy.

Set it down.

IN THE QUIET PLACES
Stories from meeting myself in quarantine and everything after
Nonfiction by Nikki Martin

March 15, 2020

Here is what I know. What I have seen confirmed a hundred times over the past week or so. Step into the practices that ground you. They matter most NOW. Yes, yoga. Or meditation. Or deep breathing. Or anything physical that reminds you to settle into the miracle of your own being. But also, reconnect to the natural world. Get grounded in the earth or by the sea or with the rising sun. Let it all take your breath away. Remind you even in the bigness of a life or of a tragedy, we are also small, a blink in the dream that is the story of time and humanity. It will all pass.

Share time with people you love near and far. Use those damn screens for something good. Use your imagination for something other than dread. Create. Paint, write, play, sing. If the things you normally rely on are out of reach, find something new. Experience a different way of stepping calmly into each and every moment.

Here is what I know. It is not fear that unites us. It is the LOVE we use to beat it back. It is the compassion we use to keep each other safe and whole of heart. It is kindness and caring and the deepest of our human yearnings, to be connected to something greater than ourselves and to each other.

Here is what I know. In some moments I am worried or afraid or steeped in uncertainty, sure. But then I pause. And I breathe. And I reach for the things that anchor me. And I remember life is always this. Filled with so much beauty, and yes, sometimes awfulness. It's who we are during both the rising of the wave to that highest crest, to the inevitable crashing down, sometimes even pulled under deep, that truly matters.

Here is what I know. I am meant to share yoga. And so as these days unfold I'll be here. Sharing. Reaching out into the world the only way I know how. With words. With yoga. And with my heart, forever longing to know it's not alone, like all of yours.

June 1, 2020

This skin. At times it's been a cage but most often it's been a home I've had to learn to fall in love with, over and over again. Through that journey, lifetimes long, only recently have I faced its color and what that meant.

You know the first time I said the words "I am a black woman," was only two years ago. Before that, it was something I never admitted because I understood I'd have to also face uneasy truths about myself, about how society saw me, about my uniqueness and sometimes aloneness, in the very communities I call home. I understood it was better to be half of myself, HALF OF MYSELF, because being my whole self meant some of what had been modeled for me, as the ideal life would be out of reach. I made choices over and over again that hid my blackness and truly believed I wasn't harming anyone but myself.

I grew up in a beautiful, loving home. With the most amazing, inspiring women. And yet, none of them had a face or skin like mine. I never talked about it but I knew they were blessed in a way I never could be and I convinced myself if I behaved the right way, and never questioned or challenged the world or the people around me, didn't make them uncomfortable with my differentness, that I could hide, I'd be accepted, I wouldn't have to worry about the same things other people of color had to.

But this is not a choice. The color of my skin. How I've hidden or celebrated it IS, however. And, I'm choosing now to stand up and own who and what I am. Racism is the same. Pretending it's not in you because of the world we've all been born into is an active choice you and many of us will have to live with. Admitting it does not make you a bad person; it makes you willing to do the difficult and challenging work of changing. Be uncomfortable. Be frustrated by the feeling that you don't have a voice right now. Remember, that is the state of POC (people of color) almost all of the time and ask yourself, in that knowing, how can you be more compassionate? How can you become an active part of the solution? How can you stand next to someone, hold them up, when they are so very tired of doing it on their own?

I'm tired. Of being afraid. Of being silent. Are you with me?

June 4, 2020

For much of my life I would proudly proclaim that I did not see color. I had a black father who also had aboriginal heritage, and a white mother. One aunt was Japanese. Another Scottish. It never occurred to me that we were any different than each other. My mom was an activist before she was twenty. She marched in some of history's greatest stories, and married a black man in 1969. They both raised me to love all people, and I grew up with friends who had histories from all over the world. I was proud that I didn't see us as different. I thought that made me part of the solution. That I could love my way to making the world better while not actually pausing to see how it was.

It took me a long time to learn that not seeing color meant I was willfully ignoring systematic racism and oppression, and I was invalidating the experience of people who did not grow up with the privileges I did even as a woman of color. I was refusing to see that sitting in love and light alone and insisting it would reach everyone equally in our society just because I saw it that way was dangerous and damaging and certainly not enough.

It was hard to face, but if we are to change the world, the work begins in our own hearts; and sometimes when we are loving and compassionate, we are the hardest to reach with difficult truths because we want so badly to believe we are good. Convincing ourselves that saving a drowning person endangers everyone on the boat is how the greedy few aboard avoid the scary work of sharing what they have. And, we are indeed complicit if we do not begin to reach out and save that soul.

So to all my "all lives..." "blue lives..." and everything in-between people: it's time to stop. You aren't wrong, but now is the time for silence except when screaming for justice. You are actively part of the problem. Just like I was. And if it's a bit scary, if it feels like you're going to lose something by giving POC and #BlackLivesMatter a voice while sitting silently on all the rest in this moment, understand that that's part of the very system we are trying to tear down. It lives in us all and it's time to do and be better.

June 8, 2020

We are at a crossroads: In the world and in the yoga community, because this community, our yoga rooms, are indeed a microcosm of the world outside our doors. Yoga is absolutely a sanctuary but it must also be a place of seeking, and truth must be at the center of that quest. Yes, this journey is first and foremost about our own inner peace and stability, but pretending it is completely separate from the outside world while we live these human lives is simply not appropriate anymore.

And so, how do we step into the work of self-reflection and seeking our own inner light while recognizing that none of us is an island in the ocean of humanity? How do we use our power, gained through practice and dedication, to make the world better and just for all, not simply ourselves?

I am going to begin with the work I'm meant to do. Helping people to sit in stillness and quietude. Helping people to land and to be present in their bodies while drawing nearer to the truth that they are so much more than that. I am going to start with myself so that I am first doing the work I'll ask others to do. Then, I'll move out into the world to offer and lead and guide. I am going to support those meant to lead the way on the path of social justice and reform. I'm going to amplify the voices that have been doing this work far longer than I have, and I'll do my best to point you towards them, too. And, I am going to hold you accountable, just as I'll work to hold myself accountable, for how we step off our mats and back into the world.

Now, more than ever, we must recognize that the solitary path towards inner peace is ultimately about peace for the whole world. None of us is truly free until we all are.

I am here. I am listening. And I am speaking up! I hope you'll join me: For the work of yoga and using it to change the world.

July 13, 2020

When the world stopped, so did I. It was shocking, the relief, to be able to pause without having to ask for it myself. And it made me think, about how I'd been moving through my life, and what I'd maybe lost in building my dream.

There are no regrets but there has been time to reflect. To rebuild with a different kind of drive. To ask myself if there can be self-love without even the gentlest self-destruction. It's been a kind of softening that challenged me to be sweeter with myself than ever before. The stillness has meant all my hard lines have collapsed. Meant some of my hard work has been given back. And yet, I'm so much happier that I marvel at how I didn't know how very run down I was before.

It's an ever-changing story. Self love in a body that's never looked the way I thought it should. And yet for the first time, it feels like it's about me and not the world. I'm still not moving or hurrying all that much. Sometimes, I do long to be what I used to be. Mostly, I feel happy I had the chance to become what I would have hurried past only a few short months ago.

July 18, 2020

I am learning to grieve the Nikkis that do not make it into this moment with me. The ones who must be left behind; not always willingly. The ones who dreamed things that will never come true. The ones with fears unrealized.

Today, I began grieving the one who pretended she was one thing while the world believed she was another. And in between those two extremes, here I am, beginning to let it all go.

July 22, 2020

The story isn't always about who we are becoming. Sometimes, it's about recognizing we aren't who we always thought we were.

I am looking at the story of myself. A woman of color who spent a lifetime hiding behind her whiteness. I wanted the privilege, the ease, the safety. I didn't know how deeply I was wounding myself. Didn't know all my suffering and struggling with a story of self love began first with self denial. Never realized, until now, that in some ways the world was just as culpable as I and yet, if change is coming, it begins here, first, inside myself.

It's not an easy thing for me to face. To know I have done harm, to myself, to others, by not stepping in to all of myself. Not when bravery is something I strive towards and yet the story of fear is what has led me here.

But, I believe in Brave Honesty also. I think it's the beginning of a fierce and authentic life. More than seeming like one thing, I am determined to BE myself: To do it as loudly or fully as I'd like and to take up space in my own heart and then fully in the world. For myself first, yes, but also because what we do within ourselves is ultimately about the kind of world we want to build. What we do for ourselves is what we become for others. I want to be a force for love and for good.

As always, thank you for reading, my sweet and beautiful friends. We are strongest when we see each other, in all our honesty.

July 26, 2020

She whispered to the wind, "if only I could love this body like I love the moon, or the stars, or the ocean waves crashing on the shore. Breath-taken and heart begging for more."

And the wind whispered back, "they are made from the very same things you are; magic and hope, and an eternal spark."

"Why can't I see it?" She cried.

As the wind hurried past, out of sight but still there, it sighed, "Stop searching for it, it's already there."

July 30, 2020

There is a part of us that remains. That always was and always will be. It is a bright spark. Brilliant. Borrowed for a little while to live a life.

There is so much more to know but that is the first and most important truth that sends us all searching in our own ways. The not knowing of it almost destroyed me when I was young; but that's a story for another day. Now, I will tell you this: Yoga is both a remembering and a forgetting all at once. What we are looking for, that Divine spark, connected to each and every other person and to its source, may be buried beneath the lessons of a life, but it is waiting, always, to be recalled and unearthed. The world is forever offering us miracles, in an infinite number of ways, to try to coax us to remember that singular truth.

Yoga taught me to listen, to look, to notice outside and within myself so that the remembering gets easier and easier. So that like on a June morning long ago when I said goodbye to my father, no matter what is going on, no matter how life is tearing you down or apart, there is a certainty to the beauty and miracle of the world, and you are not at all separate from it.

Sept 8, 2020

Once upon a time I practiced yoga to accomplish and achieve physically. No matter how my ego led me, there was a call from my heart to look deeper than all that. Over time I glimpsed a singular truth, that we aren't building anything in this practice, we are undoing, unraveling and remembering. What we are looking for is not outside of ourselves, in some ways it is not even within, because we are that which is waiting to be found and recalled and revealed.

I am still working on it all. Words are easier than truth. I should know. But this is a practice of unbecoming over time, and over and over again so I continue to show up in search of truth and myself.

I am grateful to my teacher and lineage for leading me along the way and platforms on which I get to share in honesty and humility.

Sept 20, 2020

We can't apologize for the paths we haven't walked and the roads we haven't traveled. It's tempting sometimes but it lands us nowhere. What we can do is take up the fight alongside those who have journeyed far and do so with compassion, humility, fierce determination, and love. We can trust where they tell us they've been and listen to what they say they need as allies and everyday advocates for change.

As a woman of color who also had the most amazing and privileged life, I too am learning about the gross inequities and injustices in our world. I too am learning the hard and hurtful lesson that some of my story was not as it seemed. It's tempting to apologize for being me, for not having suffered as some have, for not knowing better until now, but isn't that just more of the same? What good does it do to lament the past when we need every damn ounce of energy to fight here and now? Aren't we simply meant to do better in this moment? We are to use our voices and our platforms for change and justice and fairness and yes, LOVE, that eternal thread that ties us all together even when we are too foolish or bitter to notice it.

I can only be me. I can only step forward in my way, with my story at my back, and my truth leading me forward.

I will do and be better. I will not repeat the mistakes of the past. I am here to fight. For ALL of us. That is how I will continue to show up.

The question is: Can we be bold enough to be present?...Because this is where we will make change. This moment.

Oct 19, 2020

If we practice so that we may meet ourSELVES more fully, could it not also be so that we may meet each other more compassionately...in difference, in sameness, in conflict, in collaboration, in disagreement and in truth?

That is why I am here.

This is my yoga.

Nov 6, 2020

"You don't have to be the whole beach. Just be a grain of sand."

Earlier this week I spoke to an amazing group of Yoga Teacher Trainees about social justice and being a part of changing the world for the better, and that's what I told them...be a grain of sand. There is freedom in knowing we are small—that we are a tiny piece of a great big beautiful whole. One that is not fully formed and certainly not perfect or fair or just for all. But, we can shine. We can tend to our own sparkle and through that willingness to be, to know ourselves and to recognize our sameness (however small) with all the other grains, we can find peace. For ourselves and for each other. We can be part of the journey to finding the heart of ourselves as a whole.

To all my love warriors, spiritual leaders, peacekeepers, heart leaders, activists, yoga teachers, and more out there lending your sparkle to the world, believe it matters. You matter. Your work matters. If it didn't, the darkness wouldn't try so hard to dim your light. We shine brightest united. ALL of us, no matter our differences in belief and destiny. I will never stop fighting for us all.

Clarity
Nonfiction by Hank Dallago

I was the peacemaker. The one who wanted to be everybody's best friend. As the overly sensitive one in our family, I simply needed to be liked and accepted for who I was as I grew up. I not only wanted everyone in my family to get along, but everyone at school, too. But I was bullied at school for being shorter than most, and a person of color. My sensitivities were even more pronounced when I felt there was a conflict between me and someone else. Naturally, I needed to fix it. So, being the people pleaser, with altruistic tendencies, I would do just about anything to get people to like me or to get along. And as a result of my naïve personality, the predominant feeling I had with my dad was anxiety. Inside that anxiety was a combination of frustration and rejection. It was the one relationship in my life that I believed was broken and I didn't know how the hell to fix it.

When I began yoga at age sixteen, Dad had already served with the Navy in WWII, the Korean War, and later, in Vietnam. With a penchant for perfection and discipline, Dad was not the type to sit down with me and have a talk about feelings--neither his feelings, my feelings, nor anyone else's. He was from a generation that served their country, worked extremely hard, and did what was needed to provide for their families. He was a great man in many ways, and we had lots of family fun on fishing, camping, and vacation trips.

But as the middle child, my voice was typically drowned out by three other siblings. And it felt like Dad and I were opposites. He was working when I needed help on a school project or was resting when I needed to talk about my relationships with school friends and bullies. My sensitivity to his lack of understanding and caring were many times unbearable. So, I taught myself to play drums and percussion. Practiced yoga at home. Learned how to tell jokes to get the bullies to back off. And became a loner at school after a third move to a new town in as many years. And though Dad appeared to be interested in my life, he was also away at work for large blocks of time. Sure, Mom was there but it was not the same as talking to Dad.

Now, it was 1972 and yoga was not mainstream. Not even close. It was not popular or trendy, and exercise classes were not commercialized as they are today. Yoga practice was in front of a black and white TV screen for 30 minutes a day. With mail order instructional booklets portraying hand-sketched yoga positions, I practiced my poses on my own. The sketchbooks resembled primitive children's coloring books and consisted of about 10 to 15 poses. (Did I lose anybody there?) But here's the thing: Yoga was a big deal to me. There was a connection I made early on like a seed planted deep within my heart. I didn't know it then, but it would take years for that seed to fully grow and bloom.

Yoga began to take a turn and became my lifeline to being centered. I learned to find focus through meditation. Both yoga and meditation began to nourish me physically, mentally, and emotionally. That centeredness then became a spotlight on my self-deprecating and anxious thoughts. I created a place where I asked the positives and negatives in my life to come together. Originally, I used everything in my power to have the positives win over the negatives. My goal then was to create an understanding of who I had been in the past and remind myself of the person I was trying to become. It was my connection to something incredibly worthwhile. Something wholly personal. It felt like my yoga seed had grown, but the baggage I carried was a heavy load.

I graduated from college, married and was blessed with two children. Though, due in part to my insecurities, my marriage soon ended in a painful divorce. I dove into playing music, work, and Taekwondo to ease the pain. To minimize confusion, I read self-help books, listened to positive thinking tapes, practiced transcendental meditation, life-journaled, exercised, prayed, and somewhere in there practiced a little yoga.

Though I was still miserable, I kept looking for ways to fix myself. My yoga seed was there to grow only when I made time for yoga. Occasionally I'd find solace with passing moments of clarity and I'd try desperately to grasp the wisdom and hold on to the lessons. But they were like fleeting falling stars.

Meanwhile Dad did not offer me the emotional support I so desperately needed. We continued to share time together as a family, but not the one-on-one time my heart craved. I had so many questions and needed them answered. Dad's unwavering response to my rants were that things would work out the more I worked on them. That I could do anything I set my mind to do and needed to work harder to attain what I wanted out of life and not let things bother me so much. So, the greater I vied for his validation of who I was and who I was becoming, the less he provided. Yet, I knew he loved me, and I loved him. But the bridge between us was as wide as the Grand Canyon! Dad was great in demonstrating discipline, willpower, ingenuity, strength, and confidence. He just didn't know how to communicate or relate to me in the way I needed him to. In fact, many times his emotional silence, other than his anger, was deafening. So, the bottled-up feelings of inferiority from past mistakes, poor judgment calls, the agonizing divorce, and countless screw-ups came pouring out of me like a fire hose.

With the help of counseling, my focus was back on practicing meditation, yoga, and drumming. In time my self-image improved as well as my attitude. Then something almost imperceptible began to shift inside of me again. I didn't fully know what it was at the time and it wasn't easy for me to put into words. With time and intention, I slowly started to fit the pieces of my puzzle together. My yoga seed began to branch-out. The more I practiced mindful yoga, the more I grew stronger emotionally and spiritually. I grew up from the inside out. The effects were simultaneously subtle and overt. For the first time in my late twenties, I felt complete. Alive. Whole. It was then that the relationship with Dad changed profoundly. I finally understood that he lived his life on his own terms, and I needed to live my life on my own, too. Perhaps that is what he had tried to explain to me during our "talks" together. It felt like the maxim, "When the student is ready, the teacher appears."

In my thirties, I understood just how significant relationships are between parents and their children. The divorce left me feeling like I had lost a part of who I was, as well as the closeness to my children, as if our relationship had been fractured and couldn't be repaired. I had the nauseating feeling day and night that since I had let them down as their father, they would not want to have a meaningful relationship with me. And to add to that, I was living in a different state than my children and hadn't seen them in over six months.

One night after a practice of yoga and meditation, I had a vivid dream where my children were now adults and asked me bluntly why I had not been a part of their lives? Why did I not make the effort and sacrifice to continue to love and care for them as I committed to do as their father? I woke up from that dream in a cold sweat, and within a month moved close to them to restart our relationship. It wasn't easy to do for several reasons, but it was what I needed to do, and what I wanted to do to preserve our relationship no matter what!

My yoga seed pointed me in the direction of clarity and mindfulness, and helped me to realize how sacred family relationships should be. It was also a time to learn a powerful lesson from the relationship with my dad and carry that forward to use as a plus in my life.

Most of my insecurities have gone away. Should one come up, I only give it enough attention to test its relevance and if it has none, then let it go. My clarity is what keeps me connected to yoga and yoga connected to me. My practice that began nearly fifty years ago is now about letting go and listening to what my body needs from one practice to the next. It's my lifeline to peacefulness, mindfulness, love, and the rare connection to *samadhi* (nirvana) that brings me incredible joy.

Usually with a regular morning meditation and a yoga practice, I center my sense of wonder and send it off to the world with love and laughter. My incredible marriage of thirty years, three adult children, adopted grandson, and community all benefit from my clarity from yoga.

Dad died a few years back and with him a part of me went, too. He had become my mentor and my moral compass. I learned so much more about his life and the many sacrifices he made for his family. My respect, admiration, and love for him grew immensely.

A few years before he passed, we had those long-awaited talks. Only now they were more about two adults with substantial life experiences to share with one another. We still talked about how our relationship had changed and become better over the years. We laughed and we cried. And those cherished moments will remain in my heart forever. Dad had also mellowed, and I, of course, had matured. Though I once needed his acceptance, the glimmers of love we shared made up for all those lean years combined. My yoga seed channels those sensitivities into compassion and prayers of love for my family, friends, and others whether I know them or not.

In a serendipitous moment, while going through Dad's belongings, I found a shoebox with three small hand-written notes of observations he had made about me while I was three and four years old. Reading them lit up my heart and bridged my appreciation and love for him even more.

Scraps of Clarity
Poetry by Hank Dallago

There's a soul who wishes at times
        he was not here but over there...

Well-hidden shoebox:
old letters and postcards
snapshots and drawings
on scraps of worn paper.

Wait. Handwritten notes.
A few lines jotted down
become perishable keepsakes
of his observations of me.

Closer and closer we're
connected to the past
crisscrossing through time –
a father and son homecoming.

Lasting comments I had not seen,
musings compressed over time
intersect and link a
child to a parent.

Heart-to-hearts unfinished
conversations interrupted –
understanding so clearly and
loving him immeasurably.

History of priceless impressions
extraordinary reunion of emotions
yesterday's kaleidoscope of thoughts
today's serendipitous deposits of joy.

Breath
For S
Poetry by Mitzi Cross

She held on
to the pull and strain
across her torso,
knee to elbow
toil and twist, muscle-
breath...circling inside,
circling,
circling like a buzzard
sailing on thermals,
muscular breath...
moving out the dead,
cleaning up the roads.
She took air into
her abdomen as full
moons gathered in her belly
and she pushed heat with
her growling breath. She rose
from cobra to pull
out the shame,
she faced it in the mirror,
on the mat, sweaty, red-
faced and breathless; exhale.

A tiny gargoyle crumbled
as Lot's wife looked back
and spilled dust out of her mouth,
out of her belly, she pulled
breath into her Sun
and saluted the many deaths
she left on a hill above
the Cumberland
where she breathed through
morning fog that whispered
off the river. Strong

in Warrior she turned back,
for one last look at a still lake
and she dove
into the river and swallowed
the sun.

(memory frozen in time)
June 18, 2019
Nonfiction by Justine Kaneris

In honor of all the men and women who have suffered and are suffering with Alzheimer's disease, and in special memory for my Grandfather, Clifford Joseph Gauthier, November 28, 1931-June 16, 2019. I love you.

It's so easy to grow up and stop noticing the background of the life we are living. The cool thing about my grandpa is that he never stopped noticing. He would always notice the cows along Hill Road, all the cars in a parking lot, and the flags waving in the wind. Back then I thought all this was so goofy, and would say things like, "Thanks for stating the obvious, Grandpa." Now reflecting back, he had it all right and most of us have it backwards. We notice the things that make us worry, stress, and lose sleep. Grandpa would not busy himself with such silly things; instead, he would notice the beauty that makes up the background of our seemingly mundane life.

Alzheimer's is a very interesting disease. You don't know what is happening until it's already done and in full swing. So, there's no way to stop and have the foresight to look back on your life, reflect, and take appreciation for what was and is now. All you knew before the disease took over is all you will ever know. While the people around you get older and change jobs, build new relationships, have babies and graduation parties, with Alzheimer's, the new people you meet will always be new people and the old people will always stay young. It is easy to take memories we make for granted, easy to be pushed off, and easy to "rain check" for another day.

When I look back on these past couple of months, maybe moving back to Michigan was a bad choice, maybe it was a financial burden on my family, maybe it caused me to work double-time with work and children, but the time spent here is something no one can take away from me. This time was spent well with people I love and it will forever be a part of my long-term memory, assuming I will live for a long time. These moments, these stressful, hair-pulling, crying and sleepless nights, only-for-the-morning-to-come-too-soon moments, are part of living. We all make choices, that may or may not work; and what works for some will not work for all. The people with whom we choose to spend our time may bring the most joy and comfort to the uncomfortable times in life. I chose to live here, but I did not know this time I spent with my grandpa was going to include the last memories we would make.

My grandma chose to go to a dance with some of her friends. Like any 1950s black-and-white movie, I can see a version of my younger grandma sitting with her friends in their poodle skirts and cardigans, hair cut short, maybe some "cat-shaped" black-rimmed glasses and some black-and-white saddle shoes. She and her friends gabbed away about the cute boys, wondering if any of them would ask them to dance. One by one, each of her girlfriends pairs off with a boy as my grandma sits and waits. "Of course, no one wants to dance with me." She sighs; sitting, legs swinging beneath the table while she fiddles with a napkin or maybe the straw in her glass. Soon the atmosphere changes, she can feel him looking down at her when she looks up at his extended palm.

"Would you like to dance?" asks this tall slender man. She was sure he was coming for one of her friends and was reluctant to choose her by the time he got to her table, but nonetheless she accepted his offer. Before she knew it, they were gliding effortlessly across the dance floor, his hand in hers and the other gently cupping the small of her back. His confidence on the floor took her breath away and caused her cheeks to turn a shade of pink that made the blush she had applied unnecessary. The music slowed, they embraced for one more dance, but before the people around them started to fade, the lights came on and the dance was over.

Memory frozen in time. The years that followed all happened so quickly. Marriage, first pregnancy... second, third, fourth... "Oh, Father" (referring to her local Catholic priest), "how do I make this stop? I cannot have any more children!"

Jobs came, jobs went, with excessive golfing always in between. Grandpa was always the life of the party, dashing, always with a smile on his face, except when he didn't. Like any big family, you have several perspectives of what kind of father he may have been. He was never able to write his own story in his own words because everyone else's perspectives had created his narrative. Years passed, kids moved out, retirement was upon the horizon. Big dreamer, big spender, one thing led to another, new business, responsibilities ever-growing. These decisions, these stressful, hair-pulling, crying and sleepless nights, only-for-the-morning-to-come-too-soon decisions, are part of living. We all make choices, that may or may not work; and what works for some will not work for all. Out of all the choices and decisions we make, we hope for the best. Another chapter lived. There cannot be good without the bad. Another memory frozen in time.

The children continued to grow and expanded their own families. Here were the fun parts; they ran and jumped in your lap, and they laughed at all your "dad jokes", they held tight and got to go home at night. I am told, *grandchildren are so much more fun than your actual children.*

Camping trips, canoeing, water balloon sling shots, and so many cans of Miller-Highlife. You laugh, you sing, you sleep, you eat. Life seems at ease, money comes, money goes. Chapter after chapter weave throughout the years, not knowing when the last one will appear. Years pass, somehow the children are grown, their kids have kids, and three generations later they all still gravitate to your lap, to sit and watch the ball game, to talk, to read, to pant and lick your face (those last two are the fur-grandbabies, of course). These kids will end up remembering you more than you remember them. You will look at them and think they are your own kids, that first generation that you created.

But now everything is new, every day is not reflected on yesterday or years passed, and trivial situations are now erased from your memory. Now only certain phrases are in place, and people you once knew talk to you and keep you company. The outside world watches your body deteriorate, slow down, until you are no longer responsive.

On the inside, you have so much more to say, so much to comment on and so much to bring to light; and you can't! You can't get the words out; your brain cannot send the proper signals to your tongue.

So patiently we try to remember how far back you do remember. We try to remember your memories frozen in time: Which ones are you replaying in your head, Grandpa? Is it the countless golf outings at the Elks? Is it picking up every single leaf from your back yard and making sure your grass lines are perfectly even on both sides? Are you out hunting with Jeff and Paul, or are you working around your Florida home and teaching a line-dancing class at the club? Is it Rome? Germany? Cruising across the Pacific or hiking with your family in the Gardens of the Gods in Colorado? Is it Dawn putting a "bubble" in your hair? Or, are you at a Grand Blanc High school football game, watching Jeff get a touchdown or Laurie doing flying splits? Is it Paul picking on you at a campsite or an evening out with your sweetheart admiring her pearly whites?

Whatever it is, Grandpa, we know you were in there watching for the past five years—watching us grow and live the life that you only got to see from a chair or your couch. And we know that you are still watching, proudly above, admiring the family you created with the woman that you asked to marry just after a month from that first dance. You did it, Grandpa. You did all you can and need to do. There are no more tough decisions to be made or moments to have; now it's time to rest. For real this time. Rest and watch, love and be proud. You helped create a beautiful family; rest with our Creator, and enjoy the show.

*　　　　*　　　　*

Scripture from Matthew 19:13-15
"One day some parents brought their children to Jesus so he could lay his hands on them and pray for them. But the disciples scolded the parents for bothering him. But Jesus said, Let the children come to me. Don't stop them! For the kingdom of Heaven belongs to those who are like these children. And Jesus placed his hands on their heads and blessed them before he left."

I believe that Alzheimer's is a very sad disease from the outside looking in, but when I reflect on this verse from Matthew and watching my grandfather decline throughout these past couple of months, I noticed he went into a child-like state of mind. And whether this is me trying to cope with such a horrible sickness, or fit everything into a perfect box, I see Grandpa's decline as a way to preserve his soul. He had no more worry, fear, or stress of this world by the time he left, "For the kingdom of Heaven belongs to those who are like these children. And Jesus placed his hands on their heads and blessed them before he left." I love you, Grandpa, and I'm happy you are exactly where you need to be: Feeding the seagulls and watching the flags fly.

Crowded by Loneliness
Poetry by Brendon Payne

All alone, wandering through life….

How can I can be alone when I have desperation yelling in my ear?
How can I be alone yet I stare in the face of fear?
How can I be alone if judgment is leading the way?
How can I be alone while looking through glasses of limitation?
How can I be alone and go on dates with salaciousness?
How can I be alone when I have shame following so closely behind?
How can I be alone yet I dine with betrayal?
How can I be alone if I am clothed in guilt?
How can I be alone while wearing anguish on my head?
How can I be alone and wrap up in a blanket of despair?
How can I be alone when I wear a backpack of trauma every single day?
How can I be alone yet I find comfort in envy?
How can I be alone if I sometimes dine with angst?
How can I be alone while greed is my best friend?
How can I be alone and sip on sadness when I'm thirsty?
How can I be alone when I constantly hug humiliation?
How can I be alone yet I find comfort in addiction?
How can I be alone if I cry tears of grief at night?
How can I be alone while singing a duet with anxiety?
How can I be alone and also walk in shoes of trepidation?

When I strip down and stand still. Stand truly alone. Stand with myself.
Stare at myself. Hear myself. I realize that I am no longer searching,
just feeling my way towards my purpose. The noise has been silenced.
All this time, none of those things defined me.
All this time, I am what I needed. Here I am.
All this time, my life was crowded by loneliness.

The Womb
Nonfiction by Jennie Passero

The darkened room glowed
candle flame shadows
swayed on the walls
moving to Hindu beats
the music slowed
as a soft voice broke the tempo
guiding us to child's pose

"Knees wide
big toes touch
hips back
bolster supporting chest and head"

A blanket draped across my back
like a weighted pack
my warm cheek met the felt bolster
eyelids drifted shut

Time hung framed in the moment

I felt her presence

She was stolen from me
cancer robbing her
and me of years together
her energy encircled me
transporting me back
to my first home

Curled up
in the warmth of her womb
my sanctuary
our two hearts pulsed
in her body

Past and present joined hands
a mother's connection to her child
her love dripped
sweet nectar from a flower
tears fell like petals
from the corners of my closed eyes

Her memory and my sorrow
twisted at heart's center

Here I Am
Nonfiction by Susan Emeline Bills

This picture was my view from a wide leg forward fold in my dining room yoga practice this morning. I found the view captivating. It isn't often that I glimpse my furniture upside down, but many things are upside down just now. It is good to get a different perspective. When things are turned upside down, our habitual thinking is interrupted, and we look more closely to try to make sense of familiar sights presenting differently. We may notice new details about those things we look at all the time.

That goes for thoughts, too.

I've spent a lot of my life trying to interrupt my thoughts and get a different perspective. Mostly it was about not wanting to stay anywhere long enough to feel uncomfortable. Or more to the point, not wanting to stay anywhere long enough to feel too much. If I kept moving, I could stay ahead of the deluge of thoughts that led to wriggly emotions I didn't want to sit with.

On my first big escape when I was twenty years old, I set off aboard a greyhound bus that became home to me and a couple of friends as we rambled from NY to California. With each new vista came new things to think about that allowed me to put the thoughts I was running from into archive.

There have been many benefits of this quest to outrun feelings of fear, anger, shame, sorrow, and even joy. I don't think there is necessarily anything wrong with looking to the new when the old isn't where you want to be. I have traveled to and lived in some beautiful, interesting, exciting places from coast to coast and beyond. Every trip, every move, every adventure led to new perspectives. But with every new change of scene on that bus and since then, my thoughts have followed me.

In 1985, my home was a small cubby under the eaves in a ski lodge attic in Utah. Some mornings, several snowy inches were on the one shared toilet in the hall when someone left the window above it open during the night. Years before, I lived there, and an avalanche had crashed in through that same window above the toilet. It seems the snow was determined to find a way in.

A couple of years later, I lived in a cabin in the Berkeley Hills of CA with raccoons on the roof. It was more of a shack built around a brick patio fireplace than a cabin. There were two rooms with several hinged plexiglass windows that opened up to the outside and buckled when even the slightest earthquake rolled through, which in 1989 was often. There were spaces between the thin wood walls where the air and light from outside came in freely. I liked that. The floor to ceiling brick grill formed the entire back wall of the structure and stood stable and secure in contrast to the thin wood slats and malleable plexiglass panels at the front. It was a fragile fortress, both open to the elements and grounded in place, although Berkeley's ground was often moving.

I live in Maine now. But a few years ago, I was living on a sailboat in Florida for the winter, and living on a boat with leaks and no heat involved creativity and resourcefulness. Earthquakes and avalanches were rarely a concern (as they were in California and Utah). More of the challenges were around simple tasks. Dressing and undressing often happened without fully unclothing. There was a permanent layer left in place between showers. Sleeping with a scarf and a knit hat had the advantage of providing eye coverage when the sun shined brightly through the hatch directly and inches above my head. That was on sunny days. On rainy days, the scarf was great for swabbing off the cold water drips from the hatch that had an uncanny aim for my face no matter which way I turned my head.

Nights can be seemingly endless on a cold, wet, and wobbling boat...but a clear morning often comes after a long rain. And it is glorious!

Saying *yes* to the unknown regarding living in unusual places, and hanging in through some very real challenges, has made me resourceful and resilient and grateful for all that there is to experience in this big, beautiful world. Thankfully the teachers, teachings, and practices of yoga have been with me all along. I am beginning to realize that bringing awareness and acceptance to my feelings along the way, on and off the mat, allows me to be fully alive, fully enlivened, really here in my mind, body, and soul.

And *here* is where I want to be *wherever* I am.

Hot Yoga Moment
Poetry by Susan Emeline Bills

a primordial bug buzz-hum sounds from vents blowing hot, humid,
thick air
wrapping around bodies
lying on mats circled toward the center
on a wood-creaking shining shadow floor.

this sacred space

returned to time after time by feet longing to feel themselves again,
and hands needing to spread fingers wide
and feel the weight of their bodies pressing
and backs asking to open
and soften
and eyeballs needing to melt away from closed lids.
here we lie in our separate experiences sharing breath.
in the end, a door opens
and out pours the collective sigh of so many.
together, we have returned to our own selves.

Seven Steps on My Spiral Journey Home
(YELLOW BRICK ROAD BACK TO MY OWN BACK YARD)
Nonfiction By Kitty Madden 1/7/2021

1. SENSE HORRIBLE MAGIC - If I get caught up in turmoil ("TWISTER") after consulting any source of wisdom but my intuitive "I AM" power or the PURE ENERGY of HOME (FARM IN KANSAS) then I am deliberately appointing a false energy the authority to speak for me (WIZARD WHO KNOWS ALL THE CROWNED HEADS OF EUROPE). Therefore, I fall victim to suffering the consequences imposed by that power that I fear (WICKED WITCH FLYING PAST WINDOW). This is sensing powerful, but horrible magic. I AM potentially able to make it back to the home that's been available all along through deep yogic breathing!

2. CHOOSE YOUR COMPANIONS WISELY/ CHOOSE "WISE" COMPANIONS
If I feel exhausted by my journey, I can manifest anyone or anything I wish because I AM powerful. Therefore, I can draw on all the resources I think I might need to protect myself from that tired feeling by recognizing my bright, singing, dancing intelligence (SCARECROW) aided by all the courage (LION) I can muster with deep yogic breathing! Once I accept myself as I AM right now, I can flourish with the healthy heart of my choice (TIN MAN).

3. CONFRONT AND THEN VANQUISH YOUR "DEMONS"
Once I recognize the source of my fears (WICKED WITCH) I AM at liberty to say, "Be gone, you have no power here!" (GOOD WITCH) and get back to my own pure consciousness immediately -- POOF! Each time a new judgment comes up I AM powerful enough to return to the HOME of my inner sanctuary (bright, vivid rainbow spectrum). Again, this step is purified with deep, yogic breathing!

4. YEARN – Once I imagine what I need for peace (THE WHOLE RAINBOW AGAIN), then I AM empowered to return again to the home I never really left (OVER RAINBOW).

5. DREAM – Even if I lose vigilance and fall asleep on my way home and feel guilty for doing so, I AM comforted that some of my friends do, too. After all, we need to replenish our bodies with rest and it's a natural urge to indulge. The companions who dozed on the way besides Dorothy were courage (LION and TOTO, also flesh and blood). The others, TIN MAN and SCARECROW, are empty and not mortal, therefore, incorruptible. TIN MAN, as the essence of LOVE is rendered temporarily ineffectual by overwhelmed emotion, but his mortal friends are handy with his personal elixir for life – OIL CAN. In his case oil *can* after all because it represents life blood which makes him almost human, but still empty enough to fill his heart center with the breath of love he needs. I AM protected through it all by the intelligence of pure energy (SCARECROW) because it is totally restored with deep yogic breathing! Of course, TOTO (meaning totality) is ever-vigilant awake or asleep as the symbol for unceasing loyalty to HOME of pure energy.

6. SEEK – If I come upon an obstacle to my sensing pure energy (SENTRY AT THE GATE) I AM powerful enough to demand it with all my heart, courage and intelligence -- and oh, my little dogs, too.

7. SENSE PURE MAGIC -- abundance, peace, heightened sense of consciousness (OVER RAINBOW). I AM the source of pure energy -- the one who slayed the fear-inducing witch and said goodbye to all her friends whom she no longer needed for energy to manifest her wish for HOME. I can now imagine it with deep yogic breathing.

\

Mat Envy
Poetry by Yvette Huber

I'm the last to arrive
In the crowded room.
The only spot left
Is in front of the mirror.

To avoid my own gaze
I break yoga etiquette.
My eyes stray to
The reflection next to mine.

Her arms float like angel wings
To Standing Forward Bend.
My arms swing like gavels;
I sentence myself to shame.

She expertly adjusts her hips
To make her Warrior One look fierce.
I angrily clench my toes
As my sweaty feet slide apart.

She perches majestically
In Eagle Pose.
I teeter on frayed nerves
And my courage plummets.

She sails smoothly
In Boat Pose.
My arms and legs
Flail in her wake.

My jealous eyes
Follow her reflection,
Even when my head
Turns for Seated Twist.

But when I collapse
On my back for Savasana,
Her perfect image
Is no longer in view.

Yet I still hear her breath;
My mental comparisons continue.
My runaway mind jumps track
To curse the train wreck of my body.

The whistle blare grows louder.
I realize she snores!
I'm elated by the discovery!
(So un-yogi-like of me!)

I'll work on that next time.

Tantra
Nonfiction by Malcolm Glass

Holly and I slipped away from Dee Bradley's birthday party, leaving our friends jitterbugging in the garage.

"Come on," Holly said. "I want to show you something." She pulled me by the hand into the darkness under water oaks and palms.

We were in seventh grade, and both of us shy, so we were the last of our friends to pair off as a couple. My first girlfriend. Her first boyfriend. We held hands in the balcony of the Colony Theater Friday nights and kissed in the back of the band bus.

"What are you talking about?" I asked.

We ran across a dirt road and into a stand of long-needle pines.

"Something fun for us to do." Holly giggled.

In a few minutes we stumbled out of the shadows onto the starlit green of the third hole of the city golf course. At the edge of a sand trap we sat down, cross-legged, facing each other.

"Some kids were doing this in the cafeteria, but I thought it would be neat to play the game, just the two of us, alone." She smiled and took my hands.

Looking back I can see that we were kindred spirits. We had a heart connection, a spiritual bond. But at thirteen we weren't consciously aware of this; we were simply two teenagers sitting on the third green holding hands.

"Here's how you play," she said. "We stare into each other's eyes until one of us looks away. The one who holds the stare longest is the winner."

We stared. Above us, pines whispered. Holly's eyes seemed a deeper blue in the darkness. The grass tickled my legs. I almost blinked but squinted a little to hold my eyes in focus on hers. Then it seemed that her eyes were shifting back and forth. Or were my eyes drifting? Holly widened her eyes to keep them locked on mine.

I felt more nervous than the first time we kissed. My mouth was dry and my hands, clammy. I have no idea how long we held our gaze. Finally, I blinked.

"You lose," she said. We laughed.

I wiped my hands on my shorts, and she took my hands again.

"Relax," she said. "It's easier that way." She put her hand on my cheek for a moment and took a deep breath. And we started gazing at each other again.

I felt my breathing slow as I looked into her eyes. I let my face relax, and my eyes held steady without any effort. Her eyes softened. Then two owls high in the pines called to each other. We both grinned but stayed focused on each other.

We played the game over and over. Each time seemed more peaceful, and I lost sense of how long we had been gazing at each other. It seemed like hours.

We had been dating for almost six months, and for the first time I wanted to say, "I love you." But I didn't want to break the spell.

Along the way back to the garage dance, we stopped and kissed under a tall Australian oak. I looked into her eyes again and knew I didn't need to ask if she felt the same way I did.

"I love you," I whispered.

"I love you, too."

*   *   *

Years later I discovered that Holly and I had been practicing yoga that night. Eye-gazing is a basic exercise of Tantric yoga, or Conscious Loving, as many practitioners like to call it.

True to ancient Tantric tradition, Holly and I had been present for each other and solidly grounded in the moment. We had focused our attention on the other, not the self, as we glimpsed our deeper, loving selves through the gateway of the eyes. After that night we had a respect and fondness for each other deeper than most other thirteen-year-olds ever know.

Studying together, playing tennis, kissing, walking through Mead Gardens, gazing into each other's eyes, or swimming in Prairie Lake often gave us a sense of peace, security, and trust few teenagers know in the turbulent years of becoming adults. I am grateful for every moment we shared, and I often return to memories of my first love to help me find my true self when I am stressed or depressed.

The practice of Conscious Loving helps two people open to each other, to share fearlessly joys, fears, angers, and uncertainties in a bond of trust. Holly and I were too young to realize we were taking the first steps on a journey toward deep intimacy. Yet it was our innocence that made possible our soul-bonding.

*   *   *

About thirty years ago there was a renewed interest in Tantric sex. Quickly commercialized, it was touted as a way to "spice up your sex life." In truth, Tantra is not a path to better thrills of conventional sex but a path of contemplation. Also known as Sacred Sex, Tantra seeks to blend loving intimacy with meditation. Like other branches of yoga, it is a practice of breathing, energy exchange, and mindful awareness. The essence of Tantra is being wholly present in the moment, focused on one's partner.

In this kind of lovemaking, the emphasis is on the journey, not the destination. The intention of two partners is to respect, honor, and cherish the other as they allow their souls to guide them. Along the way, the sensations are similar to those of conventional lovemaking, but more prolonged and intense. Sometimes the journey ends at the usual destination of a sexual encounter. Sometimes it doesn't.

The journey is relaxed, slow, and meditative. Haste and frenetic action obliterate presence and focus. The Tantric journey is not the usual building of tension to a release, but sustaining, often for long periods of time, an exchange of sexual energy in a state of physical, emotional, and spiritual ecstasy and bliss. Sacred lovemaking seeks, ultimately, a union of two beings -- body, mind, and soul -- a metaphor, a mirror, of the union of a human soul with divine spirit.

Eye-gazing, soul-gazing, and quiet embracing are preludes to conscious lovemaking. These practices become a meditation that prepares a couple for intimacy by helping them to relax, slow down, and savor each moment they share.

Tandem and circular breathing sustain the connection of two partners through shared sexual energy, strengthening the bond in their four bodies – physical, mental, emotional, and spiritual.

Open verbal communication eliminates guessing or assuming the emotions and desires of one's partner and helps the couple open their deeper selves to each other.

Touch is at the heart of conscious loving, as in any sexual experience. Caresses and kisses, whether gentle or passionate, are spontaneous, intuitive expressions of loving and cherishing the other.

Tantra is a way to unconditional love and profound intimacy that says, "I see you, and in joy I accept who you are in this moment, in every moment."

Solace
Nonfiction by Susan Emeline Bills

For as long as I can remember I have wanted to know. At a very young age, I began to notice there was something I was connected to that had nothing to do with my biology or my life circumstances. I sensed there was a world within and beyond the world I perceived with my eyes and I set about exploring…mapless and determined to find my way. For a long time, I was completely unaware that I was already on a path and that I was never without guidance. I now know it was grace that turned my attention toward Eastern spirituality by way of music, books, workshops, meditation, yoga, and kirtan, kirtan, kirtan.

Many of the most profound moments of my life over the past 30+ years can be traced back almost directly to when I first came upon Ram Dass's writings. My heart and mind were blown open and since then in the midst of my days with all of the ups, downs, and in-betweens I have been sustained and nourished by an unimpeded flow of light into that open place.

My hope is that by sharing my thoughts and feelings I might type something along the way that resonates with someone and helps them to connect to the wisdom, love, and light that lives within us all. I want it to flow from my heart, not my head. Words can come to life with sequencing and intention (like a yoga class). It is with an intention to hold my heart and mind open to the flow of grace that I offer the following thoughts. The sequence may seem a bit meandering, but like a river, there is life energy in the flow.

Solace

Unease in body, mind, and spirit arising from this global forced seclusion is maybe a gift of grace to help us collectively overcome or explore a pervasive fear of death and a deeply rooted angst about the unknown. But, what do we ever really know for certain? It is all in flux constantly. Just as each wave of the ocean is filled with new water and anything that has been stirred up from below, each moment arises out of the deep unknown and manifests in different shapes and with different content and force every time. This place of in-between with the edges undefined is daunting. Standing on the threshold of an abyss can feel scary, but maybe it isn't an abyss but a frontier of limitless possibility.

We can't know what is coming. So many things we had counted on to continue, in the way they always had, have fallen away. We know nothing for sure other than that we are here in this moment of unknowing and having to create for ourselves a way to be sustained without many of the outward structures we had in place in our lives. It is as if the story we had written of who we are and what we do has suddenly been erased from the pages of our book. The book we thought we had written...or at least the outline we thought we had is no longer there.

What a place to begin. How to begin? How do we know the next right thing? I am defining what I need to feel purposeful in my days and looking for joy in simple things and slower ways of being.

Yesterday, I spent many minutes, many more than I would have a few weeks ago...listening to rain falling on a pile of leaves. The gentle sound evoking a feeling of all is as it should be. Simple wisdom through nature.

I am spending lots of time with the trees, really looking at the variations in bark and stature and branches and beginning, perhaps, to hear the sounds of their differences. Hearing not with my physical ears, but hearing from being in the space of the flow of their vibrations. Strange but true. So many trees. So many ways of being a tree. So many roots interconnecting to make one tree into a forest and the sky holding them.

Today, the trees spoke to me, and yesterday it was the sky.

They told me all will be well.

Solace can be found right where I am.

We.Yoga
Poetry by Jasmin Serina

Yoga practice today

Bring joy it may

For me and many

Yogis here and near me

Far away

We're merry

Breathe
Nonfiction by Lisa Sims

Breathe...Sigh
Breathe...Release
Breathe...Relax
Breathe...Loosen
Breathe...Flow
Breathe...Melt
Breathe...Weep

Reach, reach, reach
Lift, lift, lift
Ground
Long, strong, stable, balanced...hold
Curved, wrapped, bent, balanced...hold

Breathe
Just breathe
It's all about the breath
The space between each breath
With each breath, I reach for myself
Within that space, I lift myself
With each breath, I ground myself
Within that space, I find myself

Reach, reach, reach
Lift, lift, lift
Ground
Discover
Weep

I learn to love myself

Yoga has given me back my life. Yoga has given me back mySELF. Yoga has taught me that the most important relationship in my life is with myself, my heart, my spirit, my truth.

I had dabbled in yoga just enough to understand some of its benefits before I discovered Yoga Mat. I knew the next few months would be stressful at work. I knew yoga could help me manage that stress. What I didn't know was how yoga would change my life and how I saw myself.

I had grown up on horses and in dance. I began lifting weights, seriously, when I was sixteen years old. So, I already had the body awareness necessary to keep from injuring myself; I already knew what my muscles were capable of and what "too far" was for my body. Some of the asanas reminded me of ballet, especially the flow from one to the next. I loved feeling that freedom, again: the stretching, the sweeping, the lifting, the reaching, the release. So many times, I fought back tears during yoga. Why? Why in the world would yoga make me cry? I thought yoga was supposed to bring love, peace, happiness, and zen; not tears. Seriously, WTF? I'd get embarrassed and wonder if maybe I wasn't ready for yoga if I couldn't get through class without freaking crying. I mean, my god.

But...maybe this was part of yoga. I had read that yoga is supposed to be healing. Lord knows I had a LOT of healing to do. I'd been trying to heal for decades. Maybe, just maybe, yoga was the way for me to heal.

Dammit. No. I was taking yoga to help me get through the most stressful time of year for insurance people who worked with Medicare, not to get in touch with my "child" or my hippie self. I didn't have time for all that mumbo-jumbo, kumbaya crap. Jeezus Hell.

But, the people. The beautiful people I met because of yoga. It was as if a flood gate had opened and all these lovely people came rushing into my life. THEY had all that love, peace, and happiness. They showed me I could have it, too. They showed me how easy it was to obtain all of it...through yoga. They showed me yoga isn't just poses. Yoga is the breath. Yoga is gratitude. Yoga is self-care. Yoga IS love, peace, and happiness. Yoga smiles. Yoga loves. Yoga...is me. The deep-inside me. Not the superficial me. Not the clothes, the heels, the makeup, the hair (I have a LOT of hair). Yoga is my spirit, my heart, my strength, my resolve, my power...my tears.

My scars, my pain, my trauma. I thought I could yoga them away, meditate them away. Instead, they came swimming up to the surface so fast, I got the bends. Dammit. So, I had to deal with them. I'm still peeling back the layers, like Shrek's onion. I didn't get the parfait. And, I have to deal with it. Thanks to yoga, Taiji, Qigong, and meditation, I have the tools to actually deal with it. Thanks to yoga, Taiji, and

Qigong I have all these lovely people here to support me as I deal with it. Many of them are successfully dealing with the center of their onion. Some of them are still dealing with the first layer. Others are just picking at the thin, brittle, outer skin. They all have stories, empathy, and compassion to share. Our onions unite us, as does our breath.

Gum, anyone?

These beautiful people, whom I so admired, had so much knowledge and insight; they really seemed to have it together. They were also kind, loving, caring, understanding, selfless, shiny, happy people. And they actually liked me. Some of them stood before me, smiling, and said, "We're just reflecting you back at yourself. We are simply your mirror." Wait...what? So, all these people with all these amazing qualities and beautiful hearts and spirits were telling me I'm just like them? Me? I was shocked.

I'd spent so much of my life half-believing I was worthless, unlovable, unlikeable, a loser, a failure because that was the message I had received from my mother most of my life. I'm not here to bash my mom. She did the best she could with the tools she had. I understand that, now. She loves me in her way. She and I have had some wonderful conversations that led to some breakthroughs, and a lot of tears and hugs. I couldn't have had those conversations with her had it not been for yoga and the people I'd met because of yoga. However, I still hear that voice in the back of my head, telling me things that aren't true. It's not true!

Through yoga, I have learned that I AM worthwhile, lovable, and likeable. I am neither a loser nor a failure. I have so much to contribute. I have gifts and talents that are worth sharing. Healers have told me that I, too, am a healer. Me! Writers have told me that I, too, am a writer. Me! Amazing people have told me that I, too, am amazing. Me! I'm learning I can trust their judgment.

Through yoga, I have learned to connect with my breath, my spirit, mySELF. I'm in the process of creating a healthy, caring, loving relationship with myself so I can have the same kind of relationships with others. Yoga is helping me to be a better mother, grandmother, mother-in-law, daughter, and friend. Yoga is helping me to be the best me I can be. It feels pretty damn good.

Living with the Inconvenience
Speaking Out Loud: Why I Get So Angry Sometimes
Nonfiction by Justine Kaneris

The weather was decent with a slight chill in the frequent breeze. The boys were outside playing between the grass, our patio, and a little dirt trail. When they stood up, I saw that the stuffed animals and they were all very muddy, like red-red-red-southern-clay-kind-of muddy (I can hear Blake Shelton's song "Boys 'Round here" as I type this). Anyway, I am happy they were playing, using their imaginations and exploring the little piece of land they are allowed to go on.

So, life seemed just about as perfect as it could get; the kids were playing outside while Kyle was in the garage working out, and I was doing yoga on the back patio. Although, to be completely honest I still felt super irritated despite the blue skies and my alone time; nonetheless, I pushed through. The sound was an issue, but I found a solution. I twisted, I turned, I planked, I balanced, and I fell, yet I kept breathing and I followed through.

When I finished, so did the boys, and we all came inside. I had made plans, in my head, to start making dinner. However, when the boys came in, I told them they had to put all their stuffed animals in the laundry, and I did not remember that there was still laundry in both the washer and the dryer. This meant that I now had to do the laundry. Instantly, my blood started to boil and I was mad all over again. Not at the kids, not at the laundry, but at the fact that what I had "planned" on doing was changing.

CHANGE was the reason why I was mad, and inconvenience.

I had to stop what I had planned on doing to do something else. I tried to stop and slow my mind down…to think quietly to myself is difficult for me, as I am more of a verbal processor. I wondered at the root cause of this anger. I could see the look in the kids' eyes and they look worried and sad and possibly thinking, "Why is mommy mad at us? We are doing all the things she is wanting us to do?!" I see the looks, and I could feel their feels and I stopped them from pulling out the wet clothes; and bless their hearts, they were so confused. I imagine that I looked and sounded like a crazy person.

"I am sorry. This is not your fault. I should have already had the laundry taken out. You are doing exactly what I am asking you to do. I am not mad at you. I am mad because this is inconvenient and now instead of preparing dinner, I am doing laundry!" I yelled, compassionately.

After they left for upstairs, I wondered... is this why we are all mad and annoyed and sad and upset and confused? Because of change and inconveniences?

For the past week, my plans have been canceled. For example, I was stuck inside on a Monday when normally I would be at my Yoga class. And on Thursday we had a Soldier Family Readiness meeting (Army life meeting) at home on the computer instead of the planned pot-luck at the park. Then, when Saturday came along, I heard a little ding on my phone, a calendar reminder, reminding me that my best friend and her family are coming to visit, only to remind me, again, that this too, is not going to happen.

The fact is we are a country that thrives on convenience and we are now experiencing extreme inconvenience. The cool thing is we are all trying our best to manage this together. The COVID-19 pandemic is scary and real and has claimed hundreds of thousands around the world and probably more to come.

With this added pressure to stay inside with my loved ones, I am finding myself looking in the mirror more often. No, not in vain, but in reflection as to why I do what I do, and one of my reflections tells me that I get really mad at trivial things when there is a sense of change and inconvenience.

Another thing I am learning about myself is that I am very prideful and condescending when I am scared for someone I love who is hurting themselves (emotionally or physically). Instead of bringing in my interpersonal skills of understanding and compassion (which is what I would use lovingly to complete strangers), my pride gets in the way and I start giving (in my opinion) "amazing" advice to be helpful in order to "fix" them.

Subconsciously, I am thinking the same way they are, and I don't like the way it sounds out loud; nor do I like it from this point of view. So, I try to shut them down quickly and give them more positive and uplifting ways that will "solve all their problems." Even though, internally, I am acting as a hypocrite because rarely do I take my own advice. Of course, I don't want to admit defeat, I don't want anyone to feel sorry for me, nor do I want anyone to think I am depressed, so I cover it up by meeting new friends and sharing all my really good ideas with them instead.

All this on the outside looks good to strangers. However, to myself and my close friends and family I start to seem "high and mighty" as well as self-righteous. Of course, I don't want to be seen that way, so in the past I would try to pray that I would no longer be self-righteous, but it is hard to pray for something that others tell you that you are, if you can't identify this within yourself first.

So, I am working on this.

Later, I reluctantly switched over the laundry, called a friend to get some laughs, chopped up the veggies and chicken, and boiled the quinoa. I mixed it all together and used a brand-new seasoning, cardamom, that I had always been afraid to use...but hey, the good thing about change is that, with it, comes new experiences, so I can't think of a better time to try something new!

Life is a process and right now we are all in the thick of it, but at least we are all in the thick of it together, and isn't that the beauty of North America...we call ourselves the UNITED States and coming together, to work for the good of all citizens, is what we do best.

Change is scary, but it can also bring new and exciting discoveries. During a global pandemic, I think many of us can ask ourselves, *What are some good things we can discover while living in the inconvenience?*

Anchor
Poetry by Jessica R. Gibbs

The sound of water softly lapping against a stony shore,
Waves rocking my paddle board rhythmically,
Side to side,
Up and down.
My heartbeat slows
While the sun wraps me in a warm hug.
My breath and body steady,
Bobbing along the waves
As I become an anchor for myself.

Layered
A Guided Meditation by Samantha Summers

We live in a world focused on perfection, entertained by glossy social media posts that highlight moments, tiny pieces of a life. It can be easy to forget there's a lot of life lived in between: A life that may be good at its core, but also one that can be filled with heartbreak, a life that may be challenging and overwhelming. Often, we are left to manage this aspect of our lives, the behind-the-scenes version, on our own.

As a means of survival, we create layers of our personalities to help us manage all of our different roles. We fit ourselves into expectations that others have placed on us. And, if we are not paying attention, we can end up living on autopilot or living someone else's version of our life.

We can ask some questions of ourselves to help change our state of autopilot: How do we remain true to our authentic selves? At what point do we allow the need for belonging and connection to others to outweigh our own inner needs? How do we create interactions that are healthy for all those involved?

We must put in the work, the inside work. We must first fuse together our own mind and body before we can look to building those relationships with others. Putting in the work can transform our lives. Give us greater mental clarity, patience, and peace. When we connect with our authentic selves, we build a bridge for connecting successfully with those around us. It is infeasible to think we do not need layers. Yet, we can build our layers in such a way that our inner light still shines through.

As we begin our work today, let's remember we are safe in this space—that our mats are places of comfort, healing and growth.

Let's inhale deeply, feeling the breath move from the belly through the torso, passing from the throat up to the crown. Then exhaling, feeling the breath travel from the crown out through the belly.

Repeat this once, and then twice.

Clearing the mind and visualizing a set of nesting dolls, we open the first layer, that layer of fear and anxiety. Acknowledge it by specifying a particular fear, such as the fear of exclusion. Allow this fear to separate from the body. Pick it up and throw it as far into the distance as you possibly can. Feel the relief from its weight. Release a big sigh.

Moving to another layer, open the layer of regret or betrayal. Stuff a suitcase with all the pain of a particular situation. Pack it all in. See the suitcase overflowing. Now, sit on it and zip it up tight.

Imagine bringing this heavy suitcase to an airport, checking it in and then walking away. Notice how much easier it is to navigate the airport without it. Store this feeling of lightness to recall on another day.

Now, for the layer of shame. You know the one, the layer that controls all the negative self-talk. The one that says you aren't good enough, that you don't deserve anything. The one that says you're ugly, useless, and invisible. Visualize at least three of your negative go-to words on a chalkboard. Then, take the eraser and wipe them away one at a time. Take a step back and see the blank space, recognizing the opportunity to fill this space with kindness and compassion for yourself.

As we continue to open the dolls, we find the layer of grief. This grief is for our long lost dreams and goals, the ones that have not materialized for one reason or another, caught in the daily shuffle of our lives. Put these memories, lists, and books in a box. Tape it up and move it to storage. Out of sight, out of mind. Maybe it's for later, but let's start with today, the here and now.

Just a few more to go. Stay with me.

This is the layer of shrinking. It's making yourself small and not speaking up. It's hiding who you are to fit a set of circumstances. It's staying in the box someone else has created for you. Stretch the parameters with supine star. First the left arm and right leg, reaching in either direction as far as you can. Then, the right arm and left leg. Take up space.

Next, open the layer of denial or illusion. Desperate, we often lose sight of a situation. We want a different outcome, so we refuse to see the truth, refuse to see what's right before us. This desperation leads us into a spiral of unhealthy behaviors. Stop the pattern. Step off the escalator and take the stairs. Bonus: your step count will increase.

And last, but not least, we open the layer of attachment. Whether it's to places or things, we have created lives filled with creature comforts we cannot seem to do without. Envision one of yours. Think about letting it go for an hour, a day, a week, or even sharing it with someone else.

And now, find the doll that sits in the center of all the layers. Take a moment to bask in the light of your beauty, your inner work and growth. Give yourself a great big hug.

Peeling back the layers can be mentally exhausting. Let's create balance by focusing on our physical bodies for a bit, acknowledging each part, one at a time.

- Right hand, palm, back of the hand,
- Right arm, right shoulder, right ab,
- Right thigh, right shin, right foot
- Left hand, palm, back of the hand,
- Left arm, left shoulder, left ab,
- Left thigh, left shin, left foot
- Shoulder blades, spine, hamstrings, calves, heels
- Top of the head, forehead, third eye, nose, lips, chin
- Smile

Today's journey is nearly complete. As we add back the layers and prepare to return to the world outside of this space, let's consider:

- Seeking nonattachment
- Using our intuition
- Communicating healthy boundaries
- Loving ourselves
- Choosing in the space between stimulus and response
- Following our purpose and
- Finding courage in spite of our fears

Take a moment to select one of these as your guiding layer for the upcoming week.

The love and light within me honors the love and the light within each and every one of you. Together, we say, "Namaste."

The Things You Said
Poetry by Yvette Huber

The things you said followed me here
And tumbled like jacks onto my mat.
Not nimble enough to avoid the sharp points,
Nor ready to sweep the dialog away.

My arms slice through syllables in Warrior II,
But the edge of my practice feels dulled by distraction.
So I choose to invite the things you said
To move with me on my mat.

Questions tug my heart in Standing Bow.
I reach for answers with my outstretched arm.
I tuck sweet words beneath my chin in Pyramid Pose,
But they slip out when I swallow the bitter ones.

I try on a new perspective in Shoulderstand.
And calmly watch thoughts dangle from my toes.
The things you said litter my mat,
But I resist pecking through them in Pigeon Pose.

As I gain stronger presence to my practice on the mat,
I flow through the space between stimulus and response.
I will be ready to return to our conversation later
With a clearer mind and open heart.

Waking Up
Poetry by Sarah Michelle

When considering yoga and relationships, I think the first, best, worst and most intricate one we begin to discover is the relationship to ourselves. That higher driven spiritual connection and the mind that's been burned by experience is a seeming paradox. I wrote this poem at a time when I was awakening to my Divine connection, and little did I know then the significance this collection of words would have years later. Whatever your relationship to the Divine, (or the world around you) it will grow when you practice. If you haven't found it yet, or still don't know what that means, trust that it will be revealed in time.

Waking Up

The funny thing about selling your soul?
It's that you keep holding the devil accountable for what he offers...
I found the way out
Find your light
Shine it bright
Remember...
Being Divine is your birthRIGHT
Forgive yourself,
And the devil as well
Therein lies the key
To free you from hell
This contract void
Ceasing to exist.
When you find the courage to
Believe
Practice
And persist
Through the darkness
And realize
The TRUTH of humanity
Is a journey to remember YOUR connection to Divinity

To understand
As best you can
That life is Magic and Tragic
But these are the same
Duality is the Illusion
Maya is the name
We must love and forgive
Through our anger and grief
Choose to love
When emotions cut deep
I abandoned my faith
To see how far I could fall
For God to catch me
Help me rise above it all
Science and religion
Meet somewhere in between
But the first step was admitting
What wasn't working for me
God is LOVE
Isn't just a sentiment...
It's a vibrational frequency
that's felt through intent
It's praying for peace
and waves of healing sent
It's transcending
Above what I can receive
And learning to offer what I bring.
It's claiming my confidence
Making it known
I'm forgiving myself
And ready to move on
It's feeling your whole heart
Pain and all
And having the courage to admit when you fall
Because God is love
Unconditionally,
And sometimes
It's really hard for me
To remember that means
Even when
I can't forgive myself

Love myself
Understand myself
I can go within
Myself
And be loved
God is love
Love is limitless
Magnificent
And so are you.

Paddling Deep
Nonfiction by Samantha Summers

It is pouring down rain. There are so many drops and they seem to be hitting my windshield in a collective force. The windshield wipers continuously try to sweep them away, but the effort is lost. Visibility is minimal. The roads on this scenic byway are narrow, with no shoulder and a good number of curves. My hands clutch the steering wheel and I find myself leaning forward. My body is rigid, filled with tension from the task at hand.

I pass a church and realize there's a funeral in progress. So I say a little prayer for the person who has passed on to whatever lies on the other side of this world, whether it's heaven, reincarnation, or something completely different. Then I say a little prayer for myself, too.

I've been fighting this weather for a good portion of the drive and I'm headed to a paddleboard yoga class where too much wind and rain and lightning are not a good mix. I say a prayer because my soul needs the Zen which follows a practice on the water. I can feel the shift in my body just thinking about it.

I imagine being on the water. Paddle in hand, gliding with each sweep, hearing the lapping of the water against the board, feeling the continuous motion and the warmth of the sun. Inhaling the salty air and beginning to exhale the anxiety. As part of the class, we will find an inviting location on the water. Anchor and practice yoga with the sky above and water below. Focusing on the sensations unique to this practice, we will connect with ourselves and each other. And the peace within will flow.

A strike of lightning catches my attention and I attempt to concentrate again on driving. However, my mind wanders to a place in my life before I could find that Zen.

I was raised Catholic. My parents brought me to church every Sunday. I attended a Catholic elementary school and high school. I should have had a solid foundation of faith. Yet when I left for college and I began to make those decisions on my own, I started to veer away. I asked myself those questions I know so many of us have asked. "How could this all-powerful God let such bad things happen in the world?" As I grew older and my life became more complicated, I asked more personal questions. "How could God not see my struggles?" I felt lost, unheard, invisible. There was a point in my life when it all crashed in on me and I could not fight my way to the surface. I was in the water and I couldn't figure it out. The more I fought, the more things seemed to remain the same. Nothing happened. And for a while, I stopped trying, started sinking.

Then I found this yoga practice. I made a commitment to it and it has held my hand and sat with me on some pretty dark days. Yoga brought me back to life, helped me figure out how to find the surface, to release some of the anger. With every practice, I am rebuilding my relationship with God, with the universe, and with something greater. In doing so, I am also rebuilding my trust in the world. Learning to navigate the people and the things that are good for me and good to me.

As I arrive at the class location, the pelting rain turns to a light drizzle. I can see out the windshield now, and I catch a glimpse of the sun.

Dead Pictures
Nonfiction by Shana Thornton

"When you have already died, there is no more space for death," a yoga teacher says this to me when I am thirteen years old. I never forget it.

Imagine my wonder and peculiar curiosity when I discover a whole box of photographs with dead people in caskets. At nine-years old, I find that my grandmother has a dresser full of photographs: photo albums, all kinds of relatives that we have to squint to see. We have to flip most of the pictures over to read the names written on back. I've looked through these photos since I was small—one of my favorite things to do.

When she first opens those drawers, I see it as a treasure trunk. I scrutinize the faces of ancestors, and ask questions until she is stumped with a certain train of thought or family line.

I sprint away to find one of my cousins, sliding into the room on the hardwood floors in my sock feet, panting, "You have to see this! Pictures of dead people!" He follows me, maybe all of them follow me, but I don't remember. By now, the time we're adults, we've all seen the dead people pictures a few times and even shown our spouses, as a part of the family freak show, I suppose. As much as to say, "You can survive with us if this doesn't freak you out."

Most of the dead people are relatives or close, close friends of my grandparents and deserving of more than one death portrait. Can *you* imagine turning on the flashbulb and clicking? I've tried to imagine it at a funeral today. Someone taking a photo over the casket at different angles. People posing in front of the casket. *Flash*, there I am in front dressed in black one day, my Granddaddy's casket behind me: picture getting developed and penciling the Name, Death Date, Tennessee.

I shuffle the pictures around my palms, turning them mechanically, absently, one after the other, until I see my own face looking back at me. Yes, *I* have even been photographed in one of those pictures. *I'm already partially there,* the thought sinking into my body with a cool shudder, and then I run off to find one of my cousins and say, "We're in the box of pictures of dead people!" All of us, a tiny me leading the charge in front of a great-great uncle's casket with a line of cousins staring bleakly ahead, as if they might be afraid of a spanking if they don't pose with somber expressions.

My grandmother parks the car on the edge of the cemetery. "You've got to see this stone," she says. We get out and make our way across the sinking, rolling grass. She shields her eyes from the sun, scanning and searching. "It's the prettiest stone I've ever seen," she says to the landscape, as if those are the magic words to make it appear. And she spots it, to our right, a few rows over. I follow her as she moves with determination, as if we might lose a spot unless we hurry. I catch up to her, having learned to take my time, walk with presence, move my mountain. I feel her hand on my forearm, stopping me, and I follow her gaze with my own, realizing that we have arrived.

She stares into the mountain landscape on the marble—a rainbow, a waterfall, the trees reaching clouds where light breaks through. "You think Heaven looks like that?" she asks me.

I smile. "It certainly does look like heaven to me. It certainly does look like the earth to me," I say. "Heaven and earth. You think maybe we've already made it?" I ask, thinking I am clever.

"I hope not," she says. "As pretty as it can be, this hasn't been Heaven for everybody."

We don't know the woman buried there and we never say her name.

I'm sixteen and follow my cousin on a bike up a steep hill in Heidelburg, Germany. "You have to see this," he says, talking over his shoulder. "I know you'll love it."

We pedal up a hill into a forest, through a gateway where everything becomes quiet with bird song. People are tending graves of their family members, planting flower gardens. The place glows in colorful petals and lush greenery. We pass through to another section, where the graves are weedy and unkempt. The Star of David is engraved on the stones. They glow gray as ghosts. I stop the bike in the space between the two—breathing there. I snap pictures of the gravesites, the flowers springing from the seeds planted before the families were hauled off and stolen from their community by Nazis, after they were memories, and when no one would ever return from the families. The tatters of their lives cascade across the forest floor as crumbled stones, half faded dates and names, broken and jagged borders, marble sunken into earth. Later, my developed pictures become mists of dark shadows in black-and-white film, incomprehensible as the bits of histories they tried to reveal.

That day, I follow him to a WWII cemetery on the top of a tall hill where Allied soldiers are buried in neat rows. "I knew you would get it," he says at some point after a long silence between us.

"Where are we going?" my date asks. We're in college together but left class early.

"To the cemetery," I say. "You've got to see this."

"For what?"

"To take pictures so people don't forget."

"That's kind of morbid and creepy."

"Not really. There's so much history in cemeteries. Death is part of life."

I try to start yoga class and am lying on hard stone at the mouth of a cave. Inside the cave, there's a depiction of an indigenous warrior lying down. I focus on that image in my mind, and I rest in *savasana*, what is usually *final* relaxation posture, with my class.

"This is the most important posture," I say. Most of the students don't believe me, or they believe me only after they have flowed through an intense *vinyasa* class prior to the surrender into *savasana*. They think that *savasana* is to be earned. You might even say that they *believe* that idea—the earning of relaxation. Since the posture is also known as corpse pose, I realize that most people also believe that they must earn death or a death that comes with a promise earned. *What a concept*, I think, *if we were to surrender that for the alternative—that we've already died and are here to find a flow.* For this class, I begin at the typical ending.

"Let go of your orders," I say. "The final relaxation is actually first."

Singing Bowl Reflection
Photography by Beverly Fisher

– BEGINNING –
Nonfiction by Eva ten Velden

– for me and the summer of 2019 –

– THE END –

Sometimes life happens,
it takes control over my emotions,
whether I like it or not.

Staring in the distance,
I become numb to any type of sensations,
unable to realize which ones are good,
or bad.

Surrounded by undefined feelings,
I become unaware of the different relationships I am in,
unable to see which ones make me stronger,
or take away my strength.

That is when life happens,
and I let it happen.

Sometimes life happens,
but before it takes control over my emotions,
I return to my yoga mat in the Himalayas.

Envisioning the mountains,
I become aware of any type of sensations,
able to acknowledge the difference between the good or bad
and just observe.

Embracing the married couple that became my teachers,
I become to understand all the relationships I'm in,
able to realize which ones I should hold on to
and which ones I should let go.

That is when life happens,
and I decide what happens in the end.

– NOW –

My doorbell rings just when I drop my pants for a wee. *Great.* At the point of no return, I hope the mailman will still be there when I finish. In an attempt to speed the process, I contract my lower abdomen. Of course, it only slows things down.

Without drying my hands after a quick splash of water, I pick up the intercom phone. My fingers feel slippery from the soap while drops of water run down into my sleeve. The hair on the back of my neck rises and my teeth grind. *Congratulations! You are officially the least zen person of the day.* My mind mocks me but is probably not far off.

"Hello?" I ask

"Yes! It's DHL, can you please come down and pick up your order?"

"Certainly!"

I run down the stairs, barely holding my excitement. *It is here! It is here! My own yoga mat.* With a big smile, I thank the mailman and run back to my room. The box is tall, thin and, by the looks of it, covered in three roles of tape. I'm unstoppable when I slide a kitchen knife through the sticky plastic. The cardboard unfolds to reveal a bright dark blue mat.

The last few weeks, I had cleared the space in the middle of my room for this exact moment. Feeling like a kid in a candy store, I roll out the mat, take a step back and observe. It fits perfectly. *Now I just wait until my props arrive and I can start practicing.*

The mailman seems to recognize me as my blocks, balls, bolster, and strap arrive on different days spread out over the upcoming weeks. He always arrives around two o'clock, so I know at what time not to visit the toilet. With every delivery, I get more excited.

Even when I'm at university, I start daydreaming about the little yoga studio I'm creating just for me. *Oh wait, I still need to order a cleaning spray before I can start using my mat.* I pause the work on my thesis and search online for a mat cleaner. Order today, delivered tomorrow one website reads. *Good, then I'll start tomorrow.*

"What is it with people saying, *I'll start tomorrow?*" The question interrupts my train of thoughts. At the opposite side of my desk, a guy has decided to share his frustrations about people with words and no actions. We have been following the same course for a couple of weeks, but I don't believe I know his name.

Getting involved with others is still difficult, since this brought a lot of tension last year. In the process of pleasing everyone but myself, I lost a part of me. It forced me to make my world smaller. The main reason I filled my room with yoga equipment is because my world starts on the mat. There, I can truly practice reconnecting with myself and keep true to my boundaries towards others.

However, others might unintentionally show a different perspective on your life. Like this guy. Listening to his words, I realize I haven't started the thing I set out to do. I smile at him as he inspires me with the final part of his monologue: "No, don't start tomorrow. Start now!"

– BEFORE –

A soft soothing sound of wind instruments and the graceful whistle of birds came from far behind me. I looked around. The landscape I just saw had disappeared in a blurry haze. Within me, an undeniable feeling of loathing got awakened and with that, my whole body. It was the sound of my alarm.

Even though it was already past ten in the morning, it felt too early to open my eyes. Barely capable of moving, I reached out my hand to tap the snooze button on my wake-up light.

Next thing I knew, I blinked my eyes open at three o'clock in the afternoon. My heart jumped. I blinked my eyes again to make sure I saw the time right. The stress levels of last night all came back twice as high at a terrifying speed.

Without noticing, I was holding my breath the entire way from my bed to my shower. I could only think how stupid I had been to snooze and sleep through my alarm…again. The water that ran down my body was way too hot and I almost burned my skin. I didn't care enough to feel it.

The computer was still up and running. Its ventilator had been blowing its sound into my restless night with black skies and neon coloured lines of architectural drawings. My AutoCAD design had made progress when I slept. Unfortunately, that was a dream and with the lost time, I would never make the deadline.

My body couldn't cope with the pressure of my study. I was hungry all the time but felt too nauseous to eat. My muscles were sore from tension and my intestines were screaming out for help with all different types of belly cramps. I had lost at least ten percent of my weight before I broke down.

This lifestyle was dominated by Yang energy. It was off balance and needed to change. It wasn't worth it, as it didn't spark joy and wasn't healthy. I had pushed people away in order to finish my deadlines. My proud ego thought I could deal with everything on my own, but it was wrong. Now I was alone, I felt lonely, and I was in desperate need of a hug.

I paused in my project that day. After weeks of late nights and early mornings, I realized that I needed to sleep and take care of myself. It was the weekend, so there was no possibility to reach out to my tutors. I only wished they would understand and show some mercy in their tyrannical way of university teaching.

Lucky for me they did. Several phone calls made a postponement possible. A sigh of relief went through my body. I finally felt more than just stress. The winter had brought the cold into my room, so I snuggled under my duvet. I should have looked outside before and seen the dormancy of nature as a sign to take rest, but I hadn't bothered to watch. Now, I did and, within seconds, I had fallen asleep as well.

The second wake up of that day brought again an intense feeling. A feeling of self-love. I had stopped my unhealthy relationship with work and started a process of self-care. I couldn't be more grateful. However, my tense muscles clearly needed more attention, and what could be a better way to start balancing my lifestyle than with some Yin yoga? If only I had thought of that before.

– SOONER OR LATER –

"That was so good."

"Wasn't it?"

"I feel so much better now. Thank you."

"No, thank *you*," I say as I wrap my hands around my feet to give them a gentle massage. "I'm glad I could share this with you."

The sun started to set during the two-hour yoga sequence I practiced with a new friend. I met her just over ten days ago but neither one of us could have thought we would end up here together. We are sitting on the floor of her hotel room with our legs still crossed. In front of us a giant window provides a great view of the mountains under a twilight sky.

"You know, I am so happy I could come back to this village. I just don't feel safe anywhere else right now. Not that the places I have been are unsafe, don't get me wrong." The right corner of her mouth curls up and down. She stops talking to take a deep breath.

"Don't worry, I understand what you mean. Nothing here makes me want to leave. At home, my yoga mat is the only place I feel safe no matter what emotions have overwhelmed me. However, this place is something else. Like a safe little oasis in the rough mountain desert."

"Yes, right! Although, I also think it has to do with myself. I have never had an experience to feel this open. Like I'm putting myself completely out there, in an unknown environment, without having control."

"I can imagine. Our time here was all about getting to know ourselves on a deeper level. We have worked so hard to get inside, it would not make sense to close off straight away."

"No, right? And I don't want to, even though it makes me scared from time to time."

"Me neither, I even feel like I need a bigger opening because I cannot yet see what it is that makes me Me."

"Yeah." My friend sighs. The trembling of her lips hasn't stopped, and she is rocking herself back and forth. "I get that, but I really need the sound of Veerle's voice to be able to do so. She is the only teacher that has made me feel this way... ever."

I say nothing while crawling off my mat onto hers. She gladly receives the embrace I offer. As I feel her warm breath over my shoulder, her body calms down.

"It is like..." A pause follows as she tries to find the right words. "Like, as if Veerle has brought a key to open your heart. Even if you don't realize she has given you this key, you will unlock your true self sooner or later."

– EARLIER –

Wait a minute. The thought came up somewhere from the back of my mind. I didn't expect it. My unconsciousness apparently became in conscious need of a break, since my whole being was overwhelmed. In my head, the air had become heavy with thoughts and the sky dark with negative clouds. These clouds used to be waiting. Waiting to burst, to pour out my judgment over the person in front of me.

More often than not, I have let them. Although I didn't exactly let them, they instigated a mutiny and took over control. When they did, a deep feeling would arise from my core. I haven't been able to define this feeling yet. It varied too often. The only thing I knew was that the strength it arrived with frightened me.

The clouds mostly arrived during a conversation with a person close to me. The conversation might be unpleasant, unfair, or even harsh. However, my intention never was to bring harm with my response. Nonetheless, did my lips speak words faster than my thoughts had processed them. In my mind, there was no room for observation. I had to speak my truth and react right away.

Something changed this time. There were heavy thoughts and negative clouds. They were there, but they weren't waiting to burst. Instead, they were waiting to pass by. They just needed me to wait with them. Wait a minute.

I kept quiet and closed my eyes. A slight cool tickling started from the tip of my nose. I could feel the moisture on my skin above my upper lip. The area around my throat became dry and changed in temperature. As my chest rose, my posture became taller and even my lower abdomen expanded.

Then, I paused for a few seconds and experienced a sense of complete fullness. My mind loosened itself from the heavy thoughts. However, before I became completely lightheaded, I stopped my pause and continued. I emptied out all that just arose, all I had filled.

Everything had to go, the heavy thoughts, the negativity, the judgment, the deep core feeling, the pain, the tears. All of it flew out. I heard a soft ocean sound as the tickling at the tip of my nose was slightly warmer. My posture became smaller but still upright and strong. I paused again to observe the spaciousness and be present. I started over while I opened my eyes.

The clouds were gone, and a bright light brought me back to the conversation I had just tuned out. I needed to speak my truth, but as it turned out, my true truth was only to be found through a full yogic breath.

This mindful breath calmed my thoughts. It brought me a truth to stay close to the loved ones before me, where I would otherwise push them away. Sometimes I still struggled with letting go. I knew I needed a continuing yoga practice to guide and develop myself further. However, when I did manage, I could feel a sense of growth, especially since I knew I could not have taken this action earlier.

– NEXT –

"Tell me. How have you been?" Metal scratches against the ceramic plates while light blue eyes pierce my way. I look back, but I cannot hold for long. She knows me too well, and I don't want to tear up before even having swallowed one bite of the meal in front of me.

"Oh, you know, the usual." I try to keep the conversation light. We haven't seen each other for a long time and the last thing we need are heavy words to surround us.

"The usual?" Above the light blue eyes, an eyebrow frowns up. I should have expected that. Of all my friends she will be the last one to fool.

"I do feel like I'm more on top of it, though." I quickly take another bite, so I don't have to respond to the next comment straight away.

"Quit the nonsense and tell me what is going on, please." There is no raise in volume or a different intonation, but I can tell my friend is serious. She patiently waits until I am ready to answer.

"Well, to be straight out honest, my heart is still aching from the breakup, my mind doesn't know how to cope with the phone calls of my mother, and I'm working so hard that my stress level hurts my stomach."

"So how exactly are you on top of things? If you don't mind me asking." My friend's question isn't out of place. There is a reason I haven't seen her for so long. I have neglected her, like I have neglected myself. My life has been so intense I had no idea how to be me and how to be with others.

"I have been practicing yoga. Two hours a day I make time for only me. I try to listen to my body. If I wake up with lots of energy, I do a vinyasa. If I need some relaxation after a stressful day at university, I choose a yin session. It is amazing how much more space I experience in my body, but mostly in my mind. I haven't skipped a day since I started. Oh, and did I tell you how good it feels? Well, it feels amazing. I even decided to join a Himalayan yoga retreat!" As I keep on explaining about my summer plans, my friend just smiles at me. "What?" I ask with a small sigh of laughter as my fork stabs into a bubbling grilled tomato.

"Nothing." She replies quickly, but not fast enough to sound unreliable. "It's just your whole energy. It lifts when you talk about your routines. I'm so happy you found a way to deal with yourself in the hectic pace of your world, and you are no longer afraid to take a break from it." Her words are heart-warming. Along with two cheeks matching the tomato, I return her question.

"Tell me. How have you been?"

"Great, as always." She answers with a playful wink.

"Quit the nonsense and tell me what is going on. I can handle it again, promise."

"Most of all, I have missed you, darling. Welcome back." We talk through our dinner without watching the time. It is nearly ten when we finish the dishes.

"Let me return to my yoga mat now. Thank you for everything. It was truly good to see you tonight," I say when I cover my shoulder with a woollen shawl, and I walk closer for a goodbye hug.

"I am so proud of you." My friend says when we are holding each other and with an extra squeeze in my shoulders, she adds. "Though your life might feel like a complete chaos, I have the impression that you are more secure, stable, and even stronger. It will be exciting to see what India will bring you next."

– AFTER –

"Be widely devoted to someone or something.
Cherish every perception and at the same time forget about control.
Allow the beloved to be itself and to change.
Passion and compassion, holding and letting go.
This ache in your heart is holy."

I was lying still at the end of a yoga class when my teacher read these words out loud. They were part of a radiant sutra from an eleventh century yogic text. The words resonated deeply within every cell of my still body.

Instantly, I kept the sentences close to my heart. Words like these would guide me in discovering my truth in life towards others. I knew Savasana was not the time to run my mind over unsolved problems or unanswered life questions. However, I couldn't stop it from monkeying around after hearing these words. I realized my mind had stopped every other thought as it turned each sutra sentence into a question.

Who or what am I widely devoted to?
Do I cherish every perception of these persons or things?
Can I forget about control around them?
Can the beloved be itself?
Can it change? Has it changed?
Do I feel passion and compassion? Should I hold on or let go?
When I decide, does my heart ache?

The teacher had stopped talking. The only movement in my body was dedicated to pump air in my lungs. My being seemed still, but my thoughts moved in all different directions. I needed to focus my mind back to my breath. With every exhalation, I felt a clearing from the back of my head to the tips of my toes. It grew even bigger with an inhale.

I will remember these questions.
    Exhale. Inhale.
I will use them when needed.
    Exhale. Inhale.
I need them to secure healthy relationships.
    Exhale. Inhale.
What about the ones I have now?
    Exhale. Inhale.
I will think about that after class.
    Exhale. Inhale.
    Exhale. Inhale.
    Exhale. Inhale.
But what about the ones I have now?
    Exhale. Inhale.
No. Savasana is now. Let thoughts come after.

– FINALLY –

"The main question in yoga philosophy, or the ultimate goal, is self-realization."

"That is such a huge topic."

"Definitely. All comes down to the questions of, who am I? What is my purpose? *And,* How can my purpose be of service?" My yoga teacher explains to me. It feels like I have become close friends with her, although we have spent just a few days together.

We are having a cup of tea in the middle of a hide-away garden. The calming sound of running water surrounds us as little streams of glacier water make their way down around us. Much welcomed sunrays peek through the willow trees after some cloudy days. Every now and then, a warm summer breeze shakes the branches above our heads which allows the sunlight to flicker in even the darker parts of the garden. Feeling a sense of gratefulness to be surrounded by all this pure nature, my thoughts go back to the questions of self-realization.

"I have heard you say these questions before and every time they make me realize how little I know about myself. It is probably a question of time, since I already feel a sense of spaciousness in my heart. As if I have received a present and I have started to take the wrappings off. I'm curious to see what it will show, however, there is also a sense of fear. A fear to discover my true self and realize all the weaknesses."

"My husband René always says: embrace your weaknesses, because therefore you will have different strengths. I believe if there is one place where people should not pretend and be open, it should be on the mat and in yoga. It should be a place where you can really be yourself. If you come with a lot of darkness, then that is okay. That is welcome, because that is where you are in life."

We keep silent for a minute to let the words of the conversation sink in. Somewhere in the distance a tiny bird with a bright orange tail flies from branch to branch of neighboring trees. I watch its fluid movements as I sip some more tea.

"As yoga teachers we often see the impact a practice can have on people. Do you resonate with that?"

"Very much to be honest. Recently, I realized I was living a life that didn't make me as happy as it used to make me. Instead, I felt more and more pressure of what people and society expected of me. I had created a way of living that made me insecure and that would push me down with even slight setback. All that I thought I was as a person was suddenly nowhere to be found near me. I didn't know how to be me. It was only whenever I practiced yoga that I gave myself my full attention and I didn't feel lost."

"I am glad you did. It is not only about getting upside down for a headstand. Asanas are part of yoga, but it is really a way to tune in with yourself and take time to feel the needs of your body and mind. After all, the most important relationship we have in life is that one which we have with ourselves."

"The specific answers to the questions Who am I? What is my purpose? and How can my purpose be of service? might not be completely known to me yet, but I feel like I have learned to listen to myself finally."

– AGAIN –

Sometimes life brings me places,
with new senses I don't know,
whether I like it or not.

Staring in the unknown,
I become uncomfortable when a door gets shut behind me,
unable to see how to get out,
or feel safe.

Surrounded by darkness,
I become unrecognizable to the people around me,
unable to feel my own truth,
or that of others.

That is when life brings me places,
where I don't want to be.

Sometimes life brings me places,
but without judging the senses that occur,
I welcome the unknown.

Envisioning all that will surround me,
I become open to a comfortable seat,
able to invite myself in,
by feeling safe.

Embracing the teacher within me,
I become the true version of myself,
able to realize what it is that makes me who I am
and how that will serve others.

That is when life brings me places
that I know I will visit again.

Deep Breath
Nonfiction by Justine Kaneris

Deep breath in. Hold it. Let it all out.

"Stand tall with your legs mat-width apart.
Hands come in to heart center."

"Set your intention."

My intention is to be present while the people around me flow through these poses.

My intention is to stay focused as an instructor when I bring forward my left foot and raise my left hand, while the students in the class bring forward their right foot and raise their right hand.

My intention is to find that tiny little spot on the ground to keep me grounded as one strong leg holds up the rest of my body in tree pose.

My intention is not to doubt myself as I try to breathe five breaths in my one and only *cool* yoga pose, an extended backbend...I'm not even sure if that's what it's called.

My intention is to be a writer for the sake of writing *and* embodying a connection through words.

My intention is not to give up on myself and trust the process.

Deep breath in. Hold it. Let it all out.

Now the shades are drawn and the music calms to a soft hum or wind instrument.

"Close your eyes and allow your body to see all of your body."

I lie here and wonder how am I going to see all of my body with my eyes closed, I lay here wondering what the inside of my toes look like, bones, blood, muscle tissue?

"If your toes are flexed, release them to the ground, let the earth pull you in, be heavy in this space."

I see my baby's toes, pressing up against my fresh c-section scar while he nurses in my bed. I feel contentment. I feel important. I feel safe. I feel loved. I feel my lips turn up and a soft smile appears upon my face I notice the music has changed and I hear the wrestling of the woman beside me.

"Slowly open your eyes and turn over to your side, rise...only when you feel ready."

I notice the word "feel." Do I feel ready to turn on my side? Do I feel ready to leave my safe space with my baby and face the reality that my babies are eight and ten years old? Do I feel ready to take on the rest of my day? The rest of my life?

"The light and the love that is within me honors the light and love that is within you."

Deep breath in. Hold it. Let it all out.

Our heads bow in surrender and together we say, "Namaste."

A Candlelight Meditation
For Dunbar Cave
Poetry by Shana Thornton

The darkness of night held the space for light.
A single flame glowing.
A single flame glowing.
The cold in the night held space for warmth.
A group embracing.
A single flame glowing.
The silence in the night held space for songs.
A voice singing.
A single flame glowing.
The expanse of the night held space for daylight.
A sun shining.
A single flame glowing.

ABOUT THE CONTRIBUTORS

Introductory Author: **SARAH MICHELLE** is an adventurer, bhakti-yogini, mother, artist, musician, poet, and freelance author. She's a California native who's planted her roots in Clarksville, TN. For Sarah, the yogic path has been a powerful ally and steady anchor throughout her adult life, helping her to cultivate a strong sense of self and a deeper connection to the universe. She is passionate about the healing it has inspired, promoting her growth and empowerment as a woman and mother. She is a registered yoga teacher and licensed massage therapist and uses her writing skills to complement her work in the alternative healing community. Her mission is to help and inspire others to heal their whole selves and to live a spiritually fulfilled life. You can read her published work as the introductory author in the third edition of *BreatheYourOMBalance* by Thorncraft Publishing.

Series Editor: KITTY MADDEN is Thorncraft Publishing's Senior Editor. She not only edits every book multiple times as a line and content editor, she also helps with strategy and overall planning for the publishing company. Kitty is known as Thorncraft's literary midwife, bringing out the best writing from all of our authors. Kitty was once a professional proofreader, nanny, and substitute teacher. She is currently a Reiki Master, practicing in Clarksville, TN. She lives in sacred woods connected to ancient, petrified coral-strewn streams. She practices continually singing healing tones, coaxing dancing waters from a Tibetan dragon bowl with Luna, a dependent, resplendent, transcending, ascending, canine Reiki Master. She is the inspiration for a YouTube channel, "Kooky Kitty and Luna C. Bass," as well as co-creator, contributor, and co-producer.

Series Editor: SHANA THORNTON is an author and the owner of Thorncraft Publishing, an independent publisher of literature in Clarksville, TN. Writing is her passion, and she is the author of three novels, *Ripe for the Pickin'* (2021), *Poke Sallet Queen and the Family Medicine Wheel* (2015) and *Multiple Exposure* (2012), as well as a children's chapter book, *The Adventures to Pawnassus* (2019). She is co-author of the nonfiction self-help book, *Seasons of Balance: On Creativity and Mindfulness* (2016). Shana earned an M.A. with Honors in English from Austin Peay State University. She was the Editor-in-Chief of *Her Circle Ezine*, an online women's magazine featuring authors, artists, and activists. Shana earned her 200-hour therapeutic yoga certification from Guiding Wellness Institute, Inc. in 2017. Shana loves to be in the forest, running trails and practicing yoga.

Edition Editor: BEVERLY FISHER graduated from the University of Memphis and Vanderbilt Law School. She has appeared on "60 Minutes" in an expose about insurance scams. She was a staff attorney for Legal Aid Society of Middle Tennessee for many years before going into private practice, retiring in 2019. She has climbed Mt. St. Helens and many Mayan pyramids, canoed countless Southern waterways, and hiked a multitude of trails. Beverly is the author of a novella, *Grace Among the Leavings* (Thorncraft, 2013), and a one-act play, *My Daddy Said "He."* She was the Volume Three Edition Editor for *BreatheYourOMBalance: Yoga & Relationships*. She is a co-creator, contributor, and co-producer of a YouTube channel, "Kooky Kitty and Luna C. Bass."

Cover Photographer: AMANDA BLOUNT is a disabled retired Army combat veteran and a Department of Defense retiree as well as a multi-genre award-winning photographer from Clarksville, TN. Amanda's photography mantra is "If it stands still long enough, I'll shoot it," but where her passion for photography leads is to her work in conservation, historical preservation, photojournalism, and activism.

She maintains a strong presence in many professional and environmental groups and raises awareness of social issues through her work. Local environmentalism is important to Amanda and, through photography and film, she wants to help bring equality to all by fighting for clean and safe environments for urban and marginalized people. Amanda is also a published writer, speaker, and credited on three films. She wishes to use film and photography to tell environmental stories from marginalized and minority communities. Amanda has a passion to teach photography enthusiasts and her life mission includes encouraging young people to tell their environmental stories from their own backyards.

She's widely known for donating her time and photos to conservation and non-profit organizations and, because of her passion for history she is preparing to leave a wide variety of her photojournalism work to the public archives.

Amanda's work has been displayed several times; most recently during the Steven A. Cohen veterans' art show held at the Customs House Museum in Clarksville, TN.

Social Media handles: Twitter: @TheNatureNut
Instagram: @AmandaBlountPhotography

CONTRIBUTING AUTHORS:

SUSAN EMELINE BILLS is finally ready to call herself a writer. She has been writing for 5+ decades in journals, in her head, on blogs, websites, napkins, leaves, her hands, scraps of toilet paper (truly!), on planes, sailboats, in cafes, under trees, on beaches, beside favorite rivers and occasionally sitting at a desk. She now lives and writes on an island in Maine where the sailboat she and her husband lived on for a few years is bobbing off the dock. She became a yoga teacher many years ago because along with writing, the study and practices of yoga have been her deepest, truest calling and given shape to all her days.

ARIEL BOWLIN was born and raised in the Puget Sound area. She graduated from Western Washington University with a Bachelor's in Spanish and worked as a contract interpreter for the State of Washington for several years. She also taught Spanish Conversation at Everett Community College. Chronic injuries led her to practice and teach Yoga and Pilates. She now lives and teaches in Tucson where she loves to hike, read, and practice Yoga in the park. She is a breast cancer survivor. Find her on Instagram as @arielbowlin

JESSE CURRAN is a poet, essayist, scholar, and educator who lives in Northport, NY. Her creative work has appeared in a number of literary journals including *Ruminate*, *About Place*, *Spillway*, *Leaping Clear*, *Green Humanities*, *Blueline*, and *Still Point Arts Quarterly*. She was the recipient of the Robert Frost Haiku Prize through the Studios of Key West (2013), a Pushcart Prize Nomination (2017), and an award from the Dorothy Sargent Rosenberg Poetry Prize (2013). She currently teaches at SUNY Old Westbury and Northport Yoga Center, where she instructs a weekly class called "Yoga and Poetry." She is the mother of two bright stars, Leona and Valentine. www.jesseleecurran.com

MITZI CROSS is a playwright, poet, novelist, and fine-art photographer. Her writing and photography have appeared in several publications throughout the South. Most recently three of her photographs appeared in the Manifest gallery's catalog titled *The New Nude*. Mitzi is a Reiki Master and a practitioner of Healing Touch. Spirit has guided her to be a conduit for healing and working specifically with sexual abuse survivors and survivors of domestic violence. She has led memoir writing, poetry and creative writing groups for over twenty years and is completely dedicated to using her writing, photography, energy medicine, yoga, guided imagery and integrative breathwork to assist others along his or her path to becoming one's authentic self.

HENRY DALLAGO: Poet and writer of children's picture and board books, Henry uses his writing skills and a professional background in percussion and drumming to compose poems and stories to infuse a rhythmic and lyrical experience. Much of his work first begins as a poem, then springboards into fiction and non-fiction stories. Henry also blends his time reading to pre-school age children with local Make Way for Books and has volunteered for years with the Tucson Festival of Books. He is a member of the Arizona State Poetry Society and the Society of Children's Book Writers and Illustrators.

JESSICA R. GIBBS fell in love with reading and writing at a young age. Besides a passion for the pen, she enjoys Stand Up Paddleboarding, Yoga, and aerial dance. Writing and movement are sources of creative expression, inspiration, and ways to understand life. Jessica was also a contributor for *BreatheYourOMBalance: Writings about Yoga by Women* (Thorncraft, 2015) and *BreatheYourOMBalance: Yoga & Healing* (Thorncraft, 2018). When not scribbling in a notebook or nose deep in a book, you can find Jessica on her mat practicing, paddling on a lake, or flying through the air. Connect with Jessica on Instagram @gibby_smalls

Over the past sixty years, **MALCOLM GLASS** has published a dozen books of poetry and nonfiction. His poems, fiction, and articles have appeared in many journals, including "Poetry" (Chicago), "Prairie Schooner," "The Vanderbilt Review," "The Linking Ring," and "The Sewanee Review." His newest collection of poems, "Mirrors, Myths, and Dreams" was released by Finishing Line Press in 2018.

YVETTE HUBER practices and teaches at Yoga Mat studio in Clarksville, Tennessee. Her work on the mat will never be done.

JUSTINE KANERIS: My earliest memory is of me with a pen in my hand. I love to write, I love to text, but what I love most is to make unique connections with people. Being a military wife has allowed me to travel and to be a part of many communities throughout the United States. It has been my privilege to see firsthand different cultures and groups within the vast amount of cities where we have resided during the past fifteen years. Along with my writing, I am a mother of two and a Certified Yoga Teacher (November 2020). I am deeply in love with the wealth of knowledge and wisdom I learned from my YTT200 (Yoga Teacher Training) and excited to incorporate it not only into my writing but also my daily life. The majority of my writing practices are spiritual and nonfiction, but on occasion I will dream of something and can't help but write it down, so maybe there will be some fiction in my future.

BARRY KITTERMAN teaches writing at Austin Peay State University where he is the fiction editor of *Zone 3 Magazine*. He is the editor of *30 Poets, 30 Poems; a Clarksville Anthology.*

KHRISTEENA LUTE is a writer and English professor currently residing in upstate New York, where she spends as much of her time outdoors as possible—running, hiking, and camping—or following whatever projects or topics interest her that week.

She earned a Bachelor of Arts degree in English from Ohio University before she became a junior high literature teacher in Yuma, Arizona. During her time as a teacher, she completed a Master of Arts degree in Elementary Education from Northern Arizona University just as the Army shipped her family across the country to Fort Campbell, Kentucky. While there, she finished both a Master of Arts in English from Austin Peay State University and a Doctorate in English from Middle Tennessee State University, specializing in American women writers from the Civil War to present.

Khristeena has written several academic chapters on Grace King, which have been published in various anthologies of literary criticism. *Finding Grace and Grit* is her first novel. *Finding Grace and Grit* (Thorncraft, 2021) is a novelization of the life of Grace King (1852-1932) intertwined with the narrative of the modern writer trying to write a doctoral dissertation about her.

Find Khristeena on Instagram, @khristeenalute, or at her personal webpage, khristeenalute.net.

NIKKI MARTIN is a yoga teacher and writer living on the east coast of Canada with her two cats, Tris and Lu. Through her own lived experience and through teaching, she has come to believe whole heartedly in the practice of yoga as one that can offer space to heal, find strength, build new habits, and provide an opportunity to take much needed time for ourselves. She is passionate about teaching to all bodies, to bringing yoga to anyone curious about its power and potency, and creating an inclusive space that all people will feel welcomed in.

Her love of stories, both reading and creating them, started very young when she realized they could be both escape and salvation for a shy, sensitive and awkward kid who always felt a little bit out of place despite having friends and being very social. She drafted her first novel in grade nine and her first feature length screenplay not long after that, and has written many of both genres since. She hopes to share her work with readers over the years and to continue to share her passion for yoga while teaching and traveling.

She is an avid reader, a daydreamer, a movie lover, a sunset chaser, a stargazer, a love warrior, a tree hugger, a beach walker, a storyteller, and an ocean soul.

She was a contributor for *BreatheYourOMBalance: Writings about Yoga by Women* (Thorncraft, 2015). She is the author of the fictional series *Awake While Dreaming*, which includes the novels, *The Beginning's End* (2021) and *A Momentary Darkness* (2018). Find Nikki on Instagram as @nikki_possibilities.

JENNIE PASSERO: I most identify as an adventurer-explorer, and I love collecting experiences. I feel like the world is mine, and I am hers. I have been writing for almost 30 years, and it is how I creatively express myself. It is a way for me to process my surroundings and experiences.

The role yoga has played in my life has constantly changed. It seems as I grow and evolve different aspects of yoga lend itself to me. When my yoga practice first found me, my main focus was asana. Asana helped me to be present in my body and learn my body. At that time, I needed to move my body, and I needed to feel the postures in my body. It helped me connect to my physical self.

As my practice expands, I have found there is a heavier emphasis on pranayama and dhyana. My body needs to be still and relaxed, and my mind needs a reset and a reprieve from itself and all the external messages it receives. Breath work and meditation have allowed me a sense of peace and knowing; it allows me to unlock the answers that are within.

Read more of Jennie's work on her blog at Amor Fati, The Soul-O Traveler here: https://jenniepassero.com/
Find her on Instagram as @thesoulotraveler

BRENDON PAYNE has been working in the wellness field for the last decade, after earning a degree in recreation programming from Hampton University. Soon after breaking into the fitness industry as a personal trainer, he created his brand, Sequel Life. It is based on the foundation that we all deserve a second chance at our best life, our Sequel Life. Over the next few years he quickly acquired several certifications including personal training, group exercise, PiYo, Yoga (RYT 500), and paddleboard (SUP) yoga. This allows Brendon to work with practitioners of all ages and levels of experience.

Currently, Brendon leads corporate vinyasa classes and continues to contribute to wellness publications. In addition, he has recently led groups of students at both the high school and college level, worked with special populations and led a 200-hour training for aspiring yoga teachers.

Brendon has a passion for teaching mindfulness, helping people rediscover self-worth and for creating practices that will encourage growth. His goal is to cultivate sustainable change. Change within people will ultimately change the world.

RACHAEL RHEE is an active duty Army Officer. She came to her mat when she returned from her deployment to Iraq in 2018. Her practice not only healed the effects of years of high impact athletic activities, but it also provided her with a yoga tribe. Her yogic community wove itself into the tapestry of her heart with its unconditional acceptance of yogis from all walks of life, body types, and levels of experience. In her world where most things in her life are mandatory, her mat is one of the only places where everything is optional. She firmly believes in the following: your practice, your choice. Rachael hopes to lead her students to what she found on her mat: the profound quiet and comfort that comes from unconditional self acceptance.

Outside of the studio and her uniform, Rachael is an avid distance runner, cook, and reader of mystery novels.

JASMIN SERINA is a registered nurse living in Tucson, Arizona. She was born and educated in the Philippines. She earned her Bachelor's degree in Business Administration, major Accounting, in her late teens. She finished her Bachelor's degree in Nursing soon afterward. Jaz migrated to the USA to pursue her nursing career. She had spent time as a health care volunteer in Cambodia and Philippines. She was a conservation volunteer in Peru. Her budding yoga journey has been inspired by her instructors, family, and friends.

LISA SIMS grew up in San Antonio, TX and Germany. While in Germany, she was blessed to travel Europe. She has also been able to visit family in Canada and Mexico. Her next travel goal is to visit more of her mother's family in Romania. Lisa, who is a K-12 tutor and teaches ESL, is also eyeing the possibility of moving to South Korea for a couple of years to teach ESL.

Yoga and meditation have played an enormous part in her ability to heal, as have Taiji and Qigong. The combination of these practices have also lead her into a healthier relationship with herself and her mother. Lisa credits her aptitude for deeply diving into these ancient practices and their teachings with her ability to reconcile with her mother; to enjoy a peaceful, loving relationship with her mom before she passed away early in 2020. Lisa also believes everything she's learned through practicing yoga, Taiji, and Qigong has helped her to be a better mother, a better grandmother, and a better version of herself. She is grateful to the teachers at Yoga Mat and Stuart Bonnington for their guidance and patience.

Rediscovering her love of and talent for writing is also a direct result of Lisa's yoga, Taiji, and Qigong practices. They are also what helped her to recognise the courage to bare herself to others through her writing. These ancient practices have done for her exactly what has been written about them for hundreds of years: revealed her true self to herself - a self worthy of love.

SAMANTHA SUMMERS enjoys traveling, jeeping and walking on the beach, but yoga is her passion. She especially loves the tranquility and challenge of practicing on the water, and the paddleboard has quickly become her favorite weekend mat. Samantha believes in the transforming power of yoga, both on and off the mat. Connect with her on Instagram @gratitude.yoga.meditation

EVA TEN VELDEN: Ever since I was little, my mind has undoubtedly known the definition of monkeying around. It would wander off to make-believe universes where I could fly, breathe underwater, or live in the depths of an unknown cave. It didn't take long before I started to write down my daydreams. I think the times when it was just me and the sound of a scribbling pen were the most mindful moments of my childhood. Even now, while living my life as an architecture student in the Netherlands, those memories make me want to keep writing. They even encouraged me to start my own little business 'The Scribbling Screw' in which I aspire storytelling through architectural spaces as well as the written word. Storytelling will always bring my monkey mind back to me. Well, that and yoga, of course, so I shouldn't have been surprised when inspiration was overflowing during my wonderful stay with Himalayan Yoga Retreats.

BOOKS BY THORNCRAFT PUBLISHING

Nonfiction

BreatheYourOMBalance: Yoga and Healing, Volume Two, Introduced by Kelsy Timas, Founder and CEO of Guiding Wellness Institute, Inc. (Spring 2018).
This second volume of nonfiction and poetry delves into the poignant journey of yoga as it heals, restores, and revitalizes life after life. Many of the contributors worked together in workshops and practices at Yoga Mat studio to infuse their work with not only the personal yoga journey, but the roots of the yoga community that connect us together as well.
ISBN-13: 978-0-9979687-2-9
Library of Congress Control Number: 2017959537

BreatheYourOMBalance: Writings about Yoga by Women, Volume One, Selected and introduced by S. Teague (October 2016).
A collection of poetry, fiction, and nonfiction that focuses on breath and balance, this volume celebrates the life-changing practice of yoga. Thirty contributors share their experiences in this first collection.
ISBN-13: 978-0-9979687-0-5
Library of Congress Control Number: 2016953726

Seasons of Balance: On Creativity & Mindfulness by S. Teague and Shana Thornton (March 2016).
Teague and Thornton share a book of creativity, meditations, affirmations, expressions of gratitude and mindfulness to help you through the seasons of life. Use this book as a creativity journal to inspire you and to prompt artistic creations.
ISBN-13: 978-0-9857947-9-8
Library of Congress Control Number: 2016931608

Fiction

Finding Grace and Grit by Khristeena Lute (2021).
New Orleans author Grace King's childhood turns from Civil War era refinement to navigating the bayous with her family on a flatboat and then emerging to a different life in New Orleans after the war. In the present day, Meredith Mandin becomes fascinated by the life of Grace King after her husband returns from the war in Afghanistan, and they begin a new direction for their family. In her debut novel, Khristeena Lute shows how Meredith and Grace risk poverty and social suicide as they carve daringly different futures than the ones society had prescribed.
ISBN-13: 978-0-9979687-7-4
Library of Congress Control Number: 2020948747

The Beginning's End by Nikki Martin (June 2021). Book Two of the Awake While Dreaming Series.
Two worlds forever tied together in dreaming and in destiny will finally find their ending. And yet, is anything truly ever done in a universe where the possibility is always that things will come back around again, and again, and again?
The Beginning's End reveals a surprising struggle even while reconnecting readers with their favorite characters from the Awake While Dreaming series, which covers the lives of Kale and Kayla in book one, *A Momentary Darkness* (2018).
ISBN-13: 978-0-9979687-8-1

A Momentary Darkness by Nikki Martin (June 2018). Book One of the Awake While Dreaming Series.
A Momentary Darkness explores the realm of fantasy by experimenting with the possibilities of alternate worlds and lives. For Kayla on Earth as well as Kale on Alpha Iridium, the two women must find their true purposes in life, while finding the courage to face the combative challenges around them. This is a story within stories that can be enjoyed by anyone who dares to wander in their dreamscape.
ISBN-13: 978-0-9979687-1-2
Library of Congress Control Number: 2017959704

The Adventures to Pawnassus by Shana Thornton (September 2019).
Journey with Luna on her Adventures to Pawnassus, where she meets the literary dogs of her time and tries to fulfill her dreams. After being abandoned, Luna finds a home close to Nashville, but her troubles are not over, and she needs the friendship of Mia & her family to inspire a belief in the future.
ISBN-13: 978-0-9979687-3-6
Library of Congress Control Number: 2019905267

Ripe for the Pickin' by Shana Thornton (2021). Book Two of the Family Medicine Wheel Series.
Ripe for the Pickin' casts the original spells behind ***Poke Sallet Queen & the Family Medicine Wheel*** (2015), Thornton's Tennessee family history of tall tales, moonshining, and secrets. Robin Ballard returns to sift through the riddles in a treasure and make her way onto the stages of Nashville's music scene, pouring what she discovers from her family's secrets and sorrows into her songs.
ISBN-13: 978-0-9979687-5-0

Poke Sallet Queen & the Family Medicine Wheel by Shana Thornton (March 2015). Book One of the Family Medicine Wheel Series.
When narrator Robin Ballard takes a writing course in college, she goes searching for her homeless father and wanders into the secret lives of her ancestors and relatives. Set in Nashville and the surrounding communities, this novel offers a glimpse into the superstitions and changes of a middle Tennessee family. Based on novel events, homework assignments, old magic recipes, drunken revelries, senile remembrances, midnight songs, some tall tales, some folk tales, and lost journals, Robin Ballard tells a *true* Tennessee family history.
ISBN-13: 978-0-9857947-5-0
Library of Congress Control Number: 2015901106

Talking Underwater by Melissa Corliss DeLorenzo (August 2015).
Authors have declared that this novel is a "literary gift" and that "book clubs will love this." Cattail, the adored beach near her coastal New England home, is Amy's place of refuge. When a mistake there ends tragically, almost destroying everything that Amy holds as sacred, she

doesn't know how she'll continue, nor mend the rift with her sister that results. *Talking Underwater* explores the balance between the elation of family summers at the ocean and the ways we navigate unbearable heartache to find new ways of being.
ISBN-13: 978-0-9857947-6-7
Library of Congress Control Number: 2015938787

The Mosquito Hours by Melissa Corliss DeLorenzo (April 2014).
One turning-point summer places the grandmother, aunt, daughter, granddaughters, and great-grandchildren in the same home. An "OnPoint Radio" suggestion as "Best Summer Reads" 2014, *The Mosquito Hours* is a multi-generational story about how the women in a family attempt to keep secrets about their desires, spirituality, and motherhood. ISBN-13: 978-0-9857947-2-9
Library of Congress Control Number: 2013957635

Grace Among the Leavings by Beverly Fisher (August 2013).
Hailed by award-winning author Barry Kitterman as "a deeply moving story, one not given to easy resolution," this historical novella is a child's perspective of the Civil War. Playwrights Kari Catton and Dennis Darling adapted the book for the stage. For information on bringing the stage play to your local theatre, contact us through our website. Visit thorncraftpublishing.com for upcoming performances.
ISBN-13: 978-0-9857947-3-6
Library of Congress Control Number: 2013938285

Multiple Exposure by Shana Thornton (August 2012).
The wars in Afghanistan and Iraq have captured the lives of the U.S. military and their families for over ten years, and Ellen Masters' husband has been repeatedly deployed. In the process, she shares her desires to connect with people and to discover her own strength by training for a marathon.
ISBN-13: 978-0-615-65508-6
Library of Congress Control Number: 2012941646

For information about authors, books, upcoming reading events, new titles, and more, visit http://www.thorncraftpublishing.com
Like Thorncraft Publishing on Facebook. Find Thorncraft Publishing on Twitter as @ThorncraftBooks and on Instagram as @thorncraftpublishing